Dispelling the Myth of Home Rule

Local Power in Greater Boston

Dispelling the Myth of Home Rule

Local Power in Greater Boston

David J. Barron
Gerald E. Frug
Rick T. Su

Rappaport Institute for Greater Boston
Cambridge, Massachusetts

Table of Contents

THE RAPPAPORT INSTITUTE FOR GREATER BOSTON, based at the John F. Kennedy School of Government at Harvard University, works with universities, public agencies, and other organizations in the region to improve the governance of Greater Boston. The Institute offers five critical resources to pursue this mission:

People: Reaching out to graduate and professional students from throughout Greater Boston, the Rappaport Institute coordinates fellowship programs that place the "best and the brightest" in meaningful policy positions in government agencies.

Research: The Rappaport Institute coordinates a wide range of research projects that provide useful information and analysis. In addition to the *Governing Greater Boston* series, the Institute issues other major reports, applied research, working papers, and case studies on a wide range of issues.

Forums: The Rappaport Institute convenes forums of all types and sizes to engage the community in open-ended conversations about the public policy challenges we face in the next generation.

Information: The Rappaport Institute web site provides the foundation of a comprehensive information resource for public policy in Greater Boston. The site (*www.ksg .harvard.edu/rappaport*) provides useful information about the region's public policy projects and organizations, as well as useful original research, calendars of events, and links to Boston-related research.

Training: Building on the Kennedy School's tradition of executive training, the Rappaport Institute offers workshops and other programs for public officials, stakeholder groups, journalists, and others.

Rappaport Institute for Greater Boston
John F. Kennedy School of Government
Harvard University
79 John F. Kennedy Street
Cambridge, Massachusetts 02138
Tel: (617) 495-5091   Fax: (617) 496-1722
www.rappaportinstitute.org

Alan A. Altshuler, *Director*
Charles C. Euchner, *Executive Director*
Phineas Baxandall, *Assistant Director*
Paulina M. O'Brien, *Program Coordinator*

Publisher's Note

Dispelling the Myth of Home Rule: Local Power in Greater Boston, by David
Barron, Gerald Frug, and Rick Su, is the third volume in the Governing Greater
Boston Series published by the Rappaport Institute for Greater Boston at
Harvard University's John F. Kennedy School of Government.

The first two editions of the Governing Greater Boston Series explored a
wide range of policy and governance challenges facing the region. The thinking
behind these editions was simple: Before informed discussions of public policy
could take place, Greater Boston's "attentive publics"—scholars, public officials,
stakeholder organizations, journalists, and ordinary citizens—needed a good
survey of issues, actors, and options in each policy area. Too often, policy discussions focus on one or two aspects of an issue without an adequate understanding of the larger context.

The 2002 edition, *Governing Greater Boston: The Politics and Policy of
Place*, offers overviews and analyses of regionalism, the environment, transportation, housing, and planning. The 2003 edition, *Governing Greater Boston:
Meeting the Needs of the Region's People*, offers overviews and analyses of governance in the state and region, civic leadership, the changing demographics of
the region, family policy, education, health care, and finance and management
issues in state and local government. All of the chapters from these collections
are available at www.ksg.harvard.edu/rappaport/research/GGB.htm.

After releasing the first two editions of the series, the Rappaport Institute
shifted its focus from broad overviews toward detailed analyses of "leverage"
issues of policy and governance. Home rule provided an ideal topic for this
sharper, more analytic approach to understanding governance.

Home rule lurks behind every important concern of Greater Boston. A local
government's policies and practices on a wide variety of issues—finance and
management, land use (including the affordable housing crisis), and education—
depend on how much authority that local government enjoys. Massachusetts
provides localities with home rule authority for a wide range of legal and policy
matters. But contrary to the myth of home rule, local authority is restricted.
Localities have little discretion over taxes, fees, and borrowing. The state government imposes a number of unfunded mandates—requirements for local policy without the necessary financial resources. Cities and towns also have
fragmented control over their public schools, an issue of central and immediate
importance to all communities. When state and local statutes conflict, localities
are subject to the state laws, even when the locality is operating within the
bounds of its home rule powers. On a broad range of issues, localities must seek

passage of home rule petitions in the state legislature, a political process that gives vast powers to representatives of other communities and that can go awry for trivial reasons.

The confusion and myths about home rule have great consequences for localities and for the larger region. The consequences can be counterintuitive. Because cities and towns lack adequate control over their own affairs, they often resist efforts to bring them into larger regional strategies for housing, transportation, the environment, and other matters that have a regional scope. Localities often lack the wherewithal to deal with many pressing concerns but resist becoming part of a process that might offer a framework for dealing with those issues. One might call this stance "defensive localism."

As Barron, Frug, and Su point out, one way to open up the possibilities for regional policy is to take the local desire for home rule more seriously, but in a way that would encourage greater regional cooperation. By giving cities and towns greater capacity, in some cases as a carrot for working together, local governments will not only be able to solve more local problems locally, but also be better able to join with neighboring communities on issues of mutual concern.

The last time that the Commonwealth of Massachusetts undertook a wholesale reconsideration of state and local powers was in the 1960s, when the state passed the home rule amendment.

The Rappaport Institute, in conjunction with Frug and Barron, are producing a more detailed study of local political authority in the City of Boston. That study, funded with a generous grant from The Boston Foundation, will provide a detailed analysis of Boston's unique home rule status. The study will not only analyze home rule in Boston, but will also provide detailed comparisons with other major American cities: Atlanta, Chicago, Denver, New York, San Francisco, and Seattle.

The time may have come for a broad reconsideration of local authority in Massachusetts. The Rappaport Institute's job is to raise issues, not settle them. We hope and expect this volume to reinvigorate the political, legal, and civic dialogue on what might be the most fundamental issue in state and local government.

Charles C. Euchner
Executive Director
Rappaport Institute for Greater Boston

Executive Summary

Massachusetts is a strong home rule state, it is commonly believed. It is, people say, a state that gives its cities and towns a great deal of local autonomy. This view is so widely held that efforts to promote regionalism in the Boston metropolitan area are often dismissed as impossible. But is this view right? Over the last two years, we have investigated whether the 101 cities and towns within the Boston metropolitan region have "home rule" in the local autonomy sense of the term. To do so, we have examined the provisions of the state constitution that purport to give home rule to Massachusetts' local governments and the numerous state statutes that grant and limit local power. We have also interviewed officials from more than half of the cities and towns in the region to find out how home rule functions in practice. The results suggest that the standard story about home rule in Massachusetts is largely a myth. Indeed, promising but largely overlooked avenues for regional reform exist that would involve expanding—rather than limiting—home rule.

Among the report's key findings are:

1. Municipalities in the Boston metropolitan region have nothing like—and, equally importantly, do not feel like they have anything like—home rule in the local autonomy sense of the term.

Officials from nearly half of the towns that we surveyed rejected the suggestion that Massachusetts is a "strong" home rule state. Even those who contended that home rule was alive and well agreed that the state gives localities too few resources to deal with costly state mandates and too little authority to deal with many of the problems that their residents would like local governments to address.

Several officials told us that Massachusetts is more hostile to home rule than other states with which they were familiar. And they are right: a review of the home rule provisions in the state's constitution, as well as the judicial decisions that have interpreted them, reveals that the state has one of the most restrictive home rule amendments in the nation.

The state's limitations on home rule significantly impact the day-to-day activities of the region's municipal officials, structuring their choices and affecting the kind of policies they can pursue. In particular:

• Massachusetts gives local governments no protection against conflicting general state legislation. Given this unlimited state power to overturn local decision making, even ambiguous state legislation tends to make local officials wary of undertaking any action that has not been expressly authorized by the state.

• Massachusetts explicitly denies local governments home rule authority over taxing or borrowing. The state also subjects its localities to a broad array of unfunded mandates. As a result, municipal officials have very little control over their budgets. Often, when they exercise the discretion they do possess, local officials have little choice other than to limit the programs that are most directly aimed at responding to the concerns of local residents.

• Massachusetts affords its towns and cities less control over land use than many people think. Local governments lack the independent power to impose impact fees or to enact a range of affordable housing regulations that have proven successful elsewhere. State law also makes it difficult for cities and towns to undertake meaningful planning efforts or to change current land use laws in ways that would promote a more community-friendly environment.

• Massachusetts gives cities and towns no meaningful role in addressing the problems that exist in their public schools. State law largely limits local government's role to approving or disapproving funding requests from school committees. Judgments about school policy are given either to the school committee or, increasingly, to the state itself.

2. Key aspects of the state constitution's Home Rule Amendment do little to empower the region's towns and cities.

The state's home rule petition process is designed to enable localities to obtain authority directly from the state. It was strongly criticized, however, because local requests often die in the state legislature due to lack of attention or objections that are rooted in statewide political concerns.

The state's home rule charter process, although helpful to some municipalities in reorganizing their governmental structures, is itself so burdensome that many municipalities do not rely on it. Tellingly, most of the region's towns and cities do not have home rule charters.

3. Home rule in Massachusetts is structured in a way that limits local power *and* frustrates regionalism.

Even though the state routinely intervenes in local affairs, it does not do so in a way that promotes regionalism. In the eyes of many of those we surveyed, Massachusetts protects home rule in a way that promotes parochialism and frustrates interlocal cooperation rather than in a way that empowers cities and towns to meet the needs of their residents.

The limited nature of home rule engenders a cautious attitude in local officials that makes them wary of innovation and worried about sharing power or resources with their neighbors for fear of placing themselves in an adverse competitive position.

The constraints on local land use and budgetary authority, given the competitive context in which municipalities in the region find themselves, create incentives for municipalities to pursue strategies that keep families with children out of town. The limits that the state places on local home rule—and not just the land use powers that the state grants to its localities—play a role in promoting this kind of local exclusionary zoning practice.

Local officials had little sense that the Boston metropolitan region comprises a shared community of interest. To the extent respondents identified with anything like a region, they tended to have in mind only the three-to-five communities immediately adjacent to them.

This report does not simply challenge the myth of home rule in Massachusetts. It suggests that a more complex understanding of home rule can open up new routes for promoting regionalism. Contrary to what many believe, municipal parochialism and competition are not inherent characteristics of Massachusetts life. Current attitudes towards regionalism and its relationship to home rule are nurtured and reinforced by the current legal structure of home rule. As city and town officials know all too well, the state has created a complex mix of grants of local power and limitations on that power, not a system of local independence and autonomy. This mix of powers and disabilities creates the constrained environment within which municipal officials operate, and it plays a major role in shaping municipal officials' judgments about the kind of coordination with other localities that is possible or desirable. The obstacles to regionalism are not simply a function of local preferences to go it alone. State-imposed limitations on home rule play a major role in inhibiting inter-municipal cooperative efforts in the Boston area.

By showing what home rule means as a legal matter, and by showing how municipal officials charged with exercising it understand the concept, this report is designed to spur thinking about how the state might empower its cities and towns to enable them to address not only local problems but regional problems. The region's problems are not solely a consequence of the state's deference to home rule, and thus creating a new regional government to supplant local authority is not the only way to solve them. There may well be areas in which greater state intervention may be needed to promote region-wide goals, but the state can also promote regionalism by responding to the widespread sentiment that the state unduly limits home rule. For example, the state can enhance local power—and relax existing limitations on that power—as a means of inducing greater regional cooperation. In this way, the state can help overcome the sense of opposition between home rule and regionalism that so many municipal officials we interviewed took as a given. To make this proposal more concrete, we offer, in the concluding section of the report, some examples of how increasing local power and fostering regionalism can go hand-in-hand.

Introduction

Sprawl, traffic congestion, environmental degradation, school inequality, racial segregation, the radical difference between prosperous suburbs and declining suburbs, the spatial division between rich and poor—the problems of American metropolitan areas are as familiar as they are serious. What can be done about them? Many observers, including most urban scholars, agree that any solution to these kinds of problems must be regional in scope. But is any kind of regional organization possible—not just a regional government but *any* kind of regional organization? The standard answer to this question is "no." And the standard justification for this answer is that the attachment to local autonomy in America is too strong for central cities and suburbs to participate together in a regional approach to urban problems. Those who talk about this attachment to local autonomy usually imagine that central cities and suburbs have local autonomy. And the term they use for this kind of local power is "home rule."

Over the last two years, we have investigated whether the cities and towns within the Boston metropolitan region have "home rule" in this "local autonomy" sense of the term. We began our investigation by defining the Boston region in the same way that the Boston Metropolitan Planning Organization defines it, a definition that includes 101 cities and towns within the Boston metropolitan area. (A map of the region as so defined is reproduced in Appendix A.) Then, we asked fourteen Harvard Law School students (the names of the students are listed in Appendix B) to undertake two tasks. The first was to explore the way the legal system currently defines home rule in Massachusetts. The second was to explore how city and town officials understand the meaning of the same term as they undertake their day-to-day responsibilities. To accomplish this second task, in the spring of 2002 the fourteen students interviewed mayors, town managers, and other key officials in every city and town that responded to our request for an interview. The result produced interviews with officials from a majority—although not all—of the 101 cities and towns. (A list of the municipalities that agreed to speak with us is set forth as Appendix C). This report summarizes the results of these two efforts.

Our findings reveal four major things about the structure of home rule in the Boston region. First, they show that the state constitutional protection for home rule does not provide the cities and towns of the Boston metropolitan region with anything like the "local autonomy" that critics usually cite as the impediment to regional solutions to regional problems. Current state law contains substantial limits on local powers. It denies local governments the independent power to tax or borrow, it prevents localities from making decisions in important policy areas, and it provides municipalities with virtually no protection against conflicting state policy. The officials we interviewed experience these kinds of limits on a day-to-day basis. Although Massachusetts is often portrayed as having a strong home rule tradition, respondents for nearly half of the cities and towns that we surveyed (45 percent) rejected that description. Several used quite strong terms in doing so, describing home rule in the state as an "illusion" (Franklin) or "overblown" (Millis), or depicting the legal structure as imposing a "very controlled atmosphere" (Holliston). A number argued that, in practice, the presumption in Massachusetts is that a locality cannot act unless it has been expressly authorized to do so by the state. This would seem to be the very opposite of the presumption one would expect to find in a state committed to home rule. Still others suggested that Massachusetts gives noticeably less authority to its towns and cities than other states with which they were familiar. Even respondents who thought that the state did provide an important degree of home rule often agreed that state law gives cities and towns too few resources to deal with costly state mandates and too little authority to deal with many of the problems they face in their communities. The survey also revealed that cities and towns are constrained by more than state law limits on their powers to act. Respondents frequently noted that they were vulnerable to the adverse impact of actions taken by neighboring cities and towns and that these actions, like those of the state, are outside of their control.

Second, despite this finding, the vast majority of local officials we interviewed regularly expressed deep attachment to home rule, and many were averse to greater regionalization for fear that it would strip their communities of home rule. The same officials who elaborated their city or town's inability to make its own decisions on matters of concern to its citizens would often, at the end, vigorously defend the importance of home rule in response to questions about the potential benefits of greater regionalism. What "home rule" might mean when defended in this way, given the recognition of the constraints on local power under home rule that so many local officials identified, will be explored below in greater depth. Suffice it to say at this point that it seems to us to represent a defense of specific state-granted entitlements, a desire to maintain the distinctive character associated with the state's different localities, and a longing for more local power rather than an overall description of the autonomy that the Boston metropolitan area's local governments actually enjoy. Indeed, some respondents suggested that the current legal structure protects home rule chiefly in the sense that it facilitates a kind of parochialism that frustrates inter-local cooperation rather than in the sense of empowering localities to address their own problems. As one official put it: "[t]here's a fierce belief that you should be self-contained." (Acton). As another explained, "There's not home rule in the sense of [power being granted by the Home Rule Amendment] but in the sense that each political entity has its own fiefdom, and heaven help you if you happen to cross the borders" (Ashland). Each of these officials emphasized the real limits on local power that state law imposes even as they testified to the strength of the local attachment to home rule in this more general sense.

Third, this report demonstrates that the state's oversight of cities and towns is often structured without regional objectives in mind, despite the fact that the state is the only entity in a position to encourage regional planning. Even when the state regulates in what it considers the best interest of the region, it tends to make decisions on its own, with the affected cities and towns having little input in the process. State interactions with localities are frequent, but they usually take the form of individual transactions between the state and a specific city or town, thereby reinforcing the political isolation of municipal governments from one another. To be sure, many local officials described their experience with the state legislature or state administrative agencies as positive. A clear majority of the respondents characterized the role of the state as "basically helpful." Nevertheless, a substantial minority (13 municipalities) characterized the state's role as "basically harmful." Respondents from a number of municipalities also observed that the state affirmatively erects obstacles to inter-local cooperation. For many local officials, then, the reliance on state authority has done little to promote what they conceive of as the regional interest.

Finally—perhaps in part for the reasons just described—virtually no respondents conceived of the Boston metropolitan region as having a common identity. To the extent that respondents looked upon regionalization favorably—as some did—they tended to identify with sub-regions within the region, areas that often encompassed no more than the several towns or cities adjacent to their own. Several respondents remarked upon how little they had "in common" with many of the municipalities in the region. Within the smaller context of these sub-regions, a slight majority of respondents characterized inter-local cooperation as "high," a substantial number characterized it as "low," and the remainder termed the level of inter-local cooperation as "medium." Not surprisingly, the subject about which cooperation on this sub-regional scale was termed highest concerned joint purchasing agreements. By contrast, topics such as traffic congestion, affordable housing, and land use planning—topics that produce the familiar regional problems set forth at the outset—were often singled out as evidencing the least amount of inter-local cooperation or as posing the greatest threat to the municipality if a regional solution were pursued.

Throughout the discussion that follows, this report highlights the limitations on the exercise of local power that the current home rule structure imposes on the region's municipalities. The reason for this emphasis is not to suggest that the state should have a significantly reduced role in influencing or determining the scope of local power. A number of officials who described the state's role as pervasive defended many of its interventions as important, even necessary. Others described the state as supplying localities with a significant amount of local discretion and room to maneuver. The reason for our focus is to call into question an oft-invoked sense that Massachusetts recognizes an unusually strong degree of home rule, a degree of home rule that is so strong that efforts to promote regional problem solving are peculiarly unlikely to succeed here. By challenging and complicating just what "home rule" means in Massachusetts, we hope the report will spur further thinking about how a different way of empowering the cities and towns of the Boston metropolitan area might address the problems affecting the region while, at the same time, enabling the region's municipalities to pursue their own local interests more effectively than is now possible. There may well be areas in which greater state intervention may be needed to promote region-wide goals. But numerous constraints on local discretion also need to be relaxed. In fact, we argue, the difficulties in overcoming the many problems that confront the Boston metropolitan region may stem less from the state's respect for home rule than from the particular ways in which state law now imposes limits on local action. Removing these limits in ways that would induce the region's cities and towns to work together strikes us as an important but underutilized means by which the state could promote regionalism without further curbing home rule.

The report is divided into three sections. The first section describes the legal structure of home rule in Massachusetts and how local officials perceive its impact on their exercise of local power. The second analyzes the effect of home rule on three specific areas of municipal governance: revenue and expenditures, land use, and education. The third addresses the implications of home rule for regionalism in the Boston metropolitan area.

1. The Legal Structure of Home Rule in Massachusetts

> *"Whatever the particular issue is, [the town] has to understand that although there is home rule, [it only exists] within this framework. It really isn't true home rule."*
>
> —Town official in Greater Boston

Home rule in Massachusetts is more than a strictly legal concept, but an understanding of it requires some familiarity with certain foundational legal provisions. Two provisions in particular are key: Article 89 of the State Constitution—better known as the Home Rule Amendment (see Appendix D for the text of the Home Rule Amendment)[1] and a state statute known as the Home Rule Procedures Act.[2] These two provisions were adopted less than forty years ago with the intention of establishing home rule as a legal matter in the state for the first time.

Massachusetts's adoption of the Home Rule Amendment came relatively late. The first wave of home rule reform in the United States started in 1875 and lasted through the 1930s. Massachusetts missed this first wave, but it joined other states in passing a constitutional guarantee of home rule in a second wave of adoptions that began in the post-World War II era. The increasing demand upon municipal governments in Massachusetts, along with the time-consuming methods of reacting to these demands through special enabling legislation, prompted the Massachusetts legislature to adopt—with important restrictive modifications—the Model Constitutional Provisions for Municipal Home Rule that had been proposed by the National League of Cities (then known as the American Municipal Association). Formally adopted in 1963 and 1965 by the Massachusetts legislature, and approved by the people in 1966, the Home Rule Amendment became effective in 1967. To complement the constitutional amendment and promote "uniform standards . . . setting forth in greater the detail the procedure to be followed" in adopting a home rule charter, the Home Rule Procedures Act was enacted by the legislature in 1966.[3]

The purpose of the Home Rule Amendment is, by its own terms, to "grant and confirm to the people of every city and town the right of self-governance in local matters."[4] The actual power granted by the Amendment can be classified in three ways: Home Rule Charter Authority, General Home Rule Authority, and Home Rule Petition Authority. The term "home rule" is used in Massachusetts to refer to all three of these features of the Home Rule Amendment. The term is also used to refer to the general concept of local autonomy embraced by the "purpose" section of the Home Rule Amendment just quoted, and we will make reference to that sense of home rule throughout the report as well. Even though these elements of home rule invoke the same term, they play dramatically different roles in shaping both the practice of municipal governance and the perceptions of the degree of local power held by those charged with exercising it.

HOME RULE CHARTER AUTHORITY

Many of the local officials we surveyed associated the primary value of having home rule with the process, set forth in the Home Rule Amendment and the Home Rule Procedures Act, for obtaining a home rule charter. To understand what a home rule charter is, some general background on local governmental charters is necessary.

A municipality's charter establishes the framework for its government. The charter defines the municipality's organization, the responsibilities of its officials, many of its powers, and its relationship to its constituents. Among the things a charter typically determines is whether a municipality is a city or a town, a classification that, in turn, affects the organization of local governance and the relationship between the municipality and the state. Under state law, cities and towns have different governmental structures. Cities are managed by a city council and an executive official (a mayor or a city manager). Towns, by contrast, preserve the open town meeting or the representative town meeting as their governing body.[5] This difference in classification is important in Massachusetts. The impact of state statutes and procedural regulations may differ depending on the municipality's classification as a city or town. Town by-laws, for example, require the approval of the state Attorney General, whereas city ordinances do not.[6]

Benefits of Home Rule Charter Authority

Prior to the adoption of the Home Rule Amendment and the Home Rule Procedures Act, local governments could not adopt charters without obtaining state legislative approval. The home rule grant changed this situation by authorizing municipalities to adopt new charters on their own; these are the charters now known as home rule charters. Notwithstanding this new option, many municipalities continue to rely on non-home rule charters. Some municipalities have "special act charters"—charters adopted by the state legislature for the municipality in question, usually at local request. These special act charters, such as the one that governs the City of Boston, often pre-date the Home Rule Amendment. Other non-home rule charter municipalities have charters adopted pursuant to Chapter 43 of the Massachusetts General Laws, a section that sets forth various "model government plans" that local voters may select.[7] This method of adopting a charter is applicable only to municipalities wanting a city, rather than a town, form of government. Finally, some towns have no charter.

These towns instead operate under "a series of general laws, acceptance statutes, bylaws, and special acts that define the town's corporate identity."[8]

Against this background, the state constitutional grant of the home rule charter-making power is not without significance. A home rule charter needs no state legislative stamp of approval to become law; it is entirely a product of local decision.[9] Home rule charters may be drafted by a locally-elected charter commission and may take effect if they win approval by a local referendum.[10] A number of respondents identified the grant of home rule charter authority as an important means by which municipalities could professionalize (Boxborough), consolidate (Cohasset), and clarify (Boxborough) their governmental structure. Several interviewees reported that their municipalities used the process to change elected positions to appointed positions without seeking state approval (Ashland). According to the Department of Housing and Community Development, the trend of home rule charters has been to consolidate the power of municipal governments. These changes include reducing the size of representative town meetings, changing traditionally elected offices to appointed status, creating or strengthening management positions, and consolidating related departments.[11] More than half of home rule charters have also added recall provisions to check elected and appointed officials.[12]

Still, if the state constitutional grant of home rule amounted only to the conferral of the home rule charter-making power, it would not be surprising to find, as we did, that many local officials regard home rule in Massachusetts as weak. The adoption of a home rule charter does not give a municipality any authority that it would not otherwise be able to obtain. Regardless of what kind of charter they possess—or even whether they have a charter at all—all municipalities can exercise the general grant of home rule authority and utilize the home rule petition process authorized by the Home Rule Amendment. Indeed, a city with a home rule charter can end up being just as constrained in its actual authority— even more constrained—than a city that traced its charter to a special act from the state legislature. The significance of the home rule charter is purely procedural. An official from Millis summed up the situation this way: "Home rule is good in terms of town organization, but in terms of taxation and regulation, it's all driven by the state." An official from the town of Franklin agreed with that assessment: "You have the right to establish your own form of government here in Massachusetts, but even that's constrained, to a certain degree, by what the [Home Rule Procedures Act] says. . . . So they say, 'well, you've got home rule.' But even though we have home rule we have to do a lot of things the way that they want [us] to do it."

Limits on Home Rule Charter Authority

As the Franklin official indicated, the degree of procedural freedom that the home rule charter-making power confers can be overstated. Many non-home rule charter municipalities that we surveyed were not eager to pursue the path for charter adoption, revision, or amendment that the Home Rule Amendment has made available. These respondents noted that it is often easier to secure charter changes from the state legislature, by special petition, than it is to adopt an entirely new home rule charter or to hold a referendum to amend an existing one. Bearing out this sentiment, as of May, 2000, only 30 of the 101 municipalities in the Boston metropolitan area had adopted a home rule charter.[13] More towns (25/79 or 32 percent) than cities (5/22 or 23 percent) had done so, perhaps because the towns perceived a need to professionalize their governance structure more often than cities, which may already have done so.[14] Most home rule charters have been adopted by towns with populations between 10,000 and 25,000.[15]

The complicated process that state law sets forth for home rule charter adoption, revision, or amendment plays a role in ensuring that the state legislative petition route for charter-definition remains attractive. The state-mandated procedure for home rule charter adoption not only requires local voters to approve the final charter in a referendum but also requires them to nominate, approve, and select a charter commission responsible for drafting the new charter. In the interest of democratic efficiency, the establishment and selection of the commission is done simultaneously. The voters are thus confronted with a ballot that first asks them whether the town should adopt a charter commission, and, if they answer "yes," continues on to ask them to select who should be on the commission.[16] Malden is one of the municipalities whose attempt to form a charter commission was denied in local referendum. A Malden official told us that the denial had more to do with the complexity of the process than a genuine local belief that a new charter was unnecessary.

The denial of Malden's charter was by no means a unique event. Between 1983 and 1993, only 25 of the 44 charter commissions that were elected statewide produced a final charter that was ultimately approved—an adoption rate of only 57 percent.[17] Thus, a locality contemplating whether to adopt its own charter locally must weigh the time and expense of the effort involved in formulating a home rule charter against the reality that the process may not produce any change in the governmental structure.

In addition to confusion about process or disagreement with the substance of proposed charter provisions, one explanation for the significant number of defeats for home rule charter proposals may be the structured rigidity of the home rule charter procedure. The process for adopting a new charter is time-consuming and can be a significant drain on a locality's resources. The charter commission is allowed to define its own internal procedure and structure, and this, in turn, allows it to hire personnel and prepare commission reports at the expense of the municipality.[18] But the process is limited by the Home Rule Procedures Act to 18 months.[19] If within that time period the commission fails to produce a charter proposal, or produces a charter proposal that is not approved by the local legislature and general electorate, all expenses are wasted.

Relatedly, the home rule charter process subjects any charter proposal to a binary yes/no approval process. If any element of the charter proposal is unacceptable to the local legislature or the electorate at large, no options are available that would allow the municipality to negotiate and change that element in order to salvage what has already been done without going through the entire charter adoption process all over again.[20] The Home Rule Procedures Act thus prevents the charter proposal from being open to debate, negotiation, or amendment once it has been denied.[21] Of course, open hearings and preliminary reports provide opportunities for the municipality to influence the drafting of the final report. Still, the mandated time frame of the home rule charter procedure provides only a limited period within which compromises can be made before the whole process is lost.

Advantages of Petitioning the State and Foregoing Home Rule Charter Authority

These state-mandated constraints might explain why eight municipalities in the region[22] sought special act charters, instead of going through the home rule charter process, *after* the Home Rule Amendment was passed. Even though a special act charter requires state legislative approval, a municipality could well decide that obtaining state approval need not be more time consuming or invasive of local control than the home rule charter process. According to several respondents, special act charters, which are initially formulated locally, often pass through the state legislature with little controversy and debate if the charter does not infringe on state power. Moreover, if there are problems with the charter that the state legislature identifies, the municipalities can be told what part to amend and be given an opportunity to do so without having to start all over. Even though the state often requires special act charters to be approved through referendum, in the end the municipal government might still have more control over the drafting, timing, and management of the charter proposal than it would through the home rule charter process, with its limited time frame and delegation of the drafting process to a separately elected commission.[23]

The state legislative petition route may turn out to be more empowering when it comes to amending a charter as well. The state constitutional grant of home rule permits home rule charters to be amended locally by referendum. The state has also granted non-home rule municipalities the permission to make charter amendments without state approval through a local referendum.[24] These grants of the power to amend a charter locally are designed to free localities from seeking out state legislative permission for changes in municipal structure that may become desirable. Yet, whether or not the amendment is to a home rule charter, state law requires that even minor local amendments be adopted through a local referendum. For that reason—and because most charter amendments proposed to the state legislature pass—many officials told us that it often seems easier to pursue the special legislation route for amendment rather than the supposedly more empowering one that the state constitutional grant of home rule purported to secure.

The referenda requirement for enacting or amending home rule charters illustrates a more general point that is critical to understanding how home rule functions in Massachusetts. The laws granting home rule power often limit local decision making in the very process of authorizing it. The charter provisions of the Home Rule Amendment, for example, do not empower municipal *governments*. Instead, the home rule charter procedure transfers the final authority for approval of a charter from the state to the municipality's constituents, bypassing municipal governments. The main control that municipal governments possess over the charter adoption process is to act in an advisory capacity to the charter commission. Unlike the special act charter legislation, the municipal government has little power over the actual drafting of the charter and lacks the ability to make changes to it without having to reject it completely. Instead, it must submit the charter commission's final proposal to the electorate for a vote.[25] Although the Home Rule Amendment makes control over the charter adoption process more "local" in one definition of the term, in other words, the definition of "local" as the voters acting in a referendum can make the process more unpredictable and less efficient than special act charter legislation. Of course, for some municipalities, having the involvement of the community in public hearings and casting votes is more than an adequate reason to undergo the home rule charter process rather than to petition the state for charter approval or amendment. For others, however, it may seem like a great burden, particularly when the issue at stake is a relatively discrete one. In such instances, the state legislative petition route—for all the risks that attend the involvement of the state in such local matters—may prove to be more inviting, even more empowering, for a local community that wishes to reorganize its governmental framework.

Finally, localities might turn to the state petition process because they have no other choice. The power to amend a charter locally does not include the power to disregard conflicting state legislation.[26] If state law dictates certain aspects of internal municipal structure that local officials wish to change, there may be no means of changing those aspects without seeking state legislative assistance. In fact, even if towns or cities are merely worried that state statutory requirements might conflict with their proposed charter changes, they may be hesitant to risk taking action locally. Local officials, therefore, do not always experience the process of obtaining state legislative permission for charter amendments as a freely chosen one. Nor, for that matter, do they always experience that process as a pleasant or empowering one. An official from Malden complained: "Every time we make a change to our charter we have to do a home rule petition, and it's a pain most times. . . . It takes too much time to get these changes through—too many stages in the process. And it's wrong that people from Longmeadow have control over what's going on here in Malden. These were internal structural changes and we still have to go before a committee because a representative not from Malden was concerned that the people didn't know about it. It's a cumbersome process and it bothers me that people can question what's best for Malden when they might not even live close to here."

GENERAL GRANT OF HOME RULE AUTHORITY

While much of the Home Rule Amendment focuses on organizing municipal government, section 6 focuses on the substance of what cities and towns may do once organized. At first blush, section 6 appears to grant Massachusetts' cities and towns the ability to exercise power in very broad terms: without any specific state legislative delegation of authority, cities and towns can exercise any power that the state legislature could lawfully delegate to them. Focusing simply on this introductory delegation of power, one might conclude that the Home Rule Amendment grants a great deal of authority to the state's municipalities. It would seem to establish a broad presumption in favor of local power. Such a conclusion would, however, be wrong.

Limits on the General Grant of Home Rule Authority

The Home Rule Amendment's broad constitutional delegation of power is limited in two significant respects. One of these limitations, largely detailed in section 7, establishes a list of topics over which cities and towns have no home rule authority. These exceptions to the municipal home rule authority are the power to (1) regulate elections; (2) levy, assess and collect taxes; (3) borrow money or pledge the credit of the city or town; (4) dispose of park land; (5) enact private or civil law governing civil relationships except as incident to an exercise of municipal power; and (6) define and provide for the punishment of a felony or to impose imprisonment. The Massachusetts Supreme Judicial Court has also carved out other areas as being of insufficiently "local" concern to fall within the general home rule grant. For example, invoking the principle that that localities lack home rule power to regulate "areas outside a municipality's geographical limits," the court has invalidated a town by-law that barred the removal of gravel from its territory because of its impact on road construction throughout the Commonwealth.[27]

These restrictions have prevented municipal home rule from conferring local autonomy, as both a survey of the relevant case law and our interviews with local officials revealed. Two of the limitations mentioned in section 7—limitations not contained in the state constitutional grants of home rule in many other states—have been particularly significant. The prohibition against levying and assessing taxes restricts a municipality's ability to generate revenue—and lack of money is one of the principal concerns of city and town officials in Massachusetts. The inability to govern private or civil relationships, a conveniently broad concept, has served to curb the exercise of municipal power in many important ways. The impact of these limitations on home rule authority is examined in more detail in later sections of this report.

Another major limitation imposed by the Home Rule Amendment has been equally important. Section 6 enables cities and towns to exercise their home rule power only to the extent their actions are "not inconsistent with the [state] constitution or [the] laws" enacted by the state legislature. The Home Rule Amendment, in other words, permits the state to overrule any local decision on any matter at any time. There is, then, no local autonomy in Massachusetts if "autonomy" means the ability to determine local policy without state control. So strong is the state's ultimate power to overrule local action that it may even deny a city or town the ability to elect its own government. As the Supreme Judicial Court has explained, home rule notwithstanding, there is no state "constitutional right to an elected form of municipal government" in Massachusetts.[28] "The state legislature's authority," the court said, "includes the power to choose to provide an appointive, rather than elective, form of municipal government."[29]

The state's virtually unlimited power to overrule local action becomes important whenever a city or town wants to exercise the power granted it by the Home Rule Amendment. A key question for a municipality contemplating such an action is whether the state legislature has enacted legislation that would conflict with its proposed policy. If the state legislature has done so, the state prevails. As an official from Medfield put it: "[The] legislature, by taking action, can preclude the local community from using the Home Rule Amendment to accomplish anything. . . . Local governments are creatures of the Commonwealth of Massachusetts. They have not been able to exercise independent authority beyond the rope that the legislature will allow them to extend themselves on."

The legal term for determining whether the state has adopted conflicting legislation is "preemption." Every state in the nation empowers its state legislature to preempt local ordinances. But many states limit preemption more than Massachusetts does. The state's power to preempt is particularly significant in Massachusetts because, as construed by the state courts, a local ordinance can be found inconsistent with state law—and thus preempted—even without a specific state statute overriding it. It is enough if the state is found to have dealt with the general subject matter in a manner that, by implication, denies local power to act.[30] Even state statutes that authorize local governments to act may be construed by courts—or interpreted by local officials—as impliedly preempting other actions that the state has not already authorized.

Local Understandings of Home Rule

Our survey revealed that, in practice, the shadow of preemption (combined with the independent limits on local power that Section 7 places on many substantive areas) produces a great deal of uncertainty about a city or town's ability to exercise home rule authority. In fact, it produces so much uncertainty that many municipalities refrain from relying on their home rule authority when they want to address a matter of concern to them. It is important to recognize that even if the Home Rule Amendment can properly be interpreted to allow the municipality to take a proposed action—that is, even if there is technical compliance with the requirements of home rule—the locality has to have the confidence to rely on its home authority to take the action it envisions. Without this confidence, the home rule power will not be invoked despite the fact that it could be. Either no action will be taken or efforts will be taken to ensure that specific state statutory authority exists for the action.

Our study of proposed local actions reveals not only that the technical requirement of home rule is lacking in many areas of local concern but also that a belief in the municipality's home rule authority over policy matters is often nonexistent. Almost half of all the responses to questions regarding home rule authority, and more than 80 percent of those that felt home rule power was not important, remarked on how much the state dominated local governance and how little room was left for them to act on their own. These responses described the lack of confidence in home rule power as stemming from two distinct but related attitudes: a cautiousness in asserting independent local power resulting from a lack of clarity about what municipalities are authorized to do and a firm belief that municipalities lack the power to act in most areas in the absence of express state authorization to do so.

The cautiousness in asserting home rule stems from the pervasive ambiguity regarding the meaning of the express prohibitions contained in the Home Rule Amendment and the scope of state legislative preemption. Municipalities often want to pass local laws that may or may not conflict with state statutes. They might want to impose sanctions on a particular activity stricter than the state imposes or regulate a subject matter in a different way. That was the case when one town unsuccessfully sought to regulate the use of pesticides when not used for agricultural or domestic purposes. Even though the town bylaw would not have permitted a use of pesticides contrary to the Massachusetts Pesticide Control Act, the question remained whether localities were impliedly barred from prohibiting the use of pesticides allowed by the state act. In this instance, the town went ahead and enacted the bylaw, but the Supreme Judicial Court concluded that the Pesticide Control Act preempted the local action, albeit only by implication.[31] Given this kind of judicial decision and the fact that the state has extensive regulations dealing with almost all aspects of local governance, it is difficult for municipalities to enact anything without questioning whether they are infringing on state policies. Court decisions dealing with preemption generate further confusion because they often rely on judicial interpretations of what the state intended to do in enacting the legislation in question—an interpretation that is hard to predict in advance.

An official from Duxbury commented on the general confusion regarding home rule authority: "I don't think most people totally understand what that authority is or what that power may be, real or perceived." Town officials of Foxborough named state preemption as one of the dominant roadblocks inhibiting their ability to take action because it is so difficult to determine beforehand what has not been preempted by state statute. When one town counsel was asked whether she ever advised town administrators to abandon a course of action because it contravened a state statute, she answered that it "was not at all uncommon" for her to do so. "Whatever the particular issue is [the town has] to understand that although there is home rule, [it only exists] within this framework. It really isn't true home rule." She added: "You can almost always trace back a connection to state statutes. If the city council asks my office, we want to pass this ordinance on x, is that all right? We have to look and see if there's state law on that that precludes us from doing anything, certain things, or are we left on our own. They trumpet the home rule idea and you would think that means you can do whatever you like. Far from it. The first inquiry has to be, what's already there and how much does it confine us."

To emphasize the degree to which state presence is pervasive, a Gloucester official said: "pooper-scooper laws are also big—that's an area where municipalities have complete authority. But how important is that?" Comments from a town official from Sherborn cast doubt on the notion that even this area is free of state interference. She suggested that it was difficult for the town to address local issues such as "dog complaints" without consulting with the state because penalties and hearings are heavily regulated by the state. Even town officials who felt home rule established a presumption in favor of local power noted the prevalence and malleability of state preemption. A Sherborn official defended the importance of home rule but commented on how difficult it is to use those powers confidently because of the prevalence of state preemption.

As a result of this ambiguity, localities, whether or not they think they may have power to take a particular action, often file a home rule petition seeking state legislative permission to act—unless, that is, they abandon their intended course of action altogether. An example comes from the town of Arlington. The town wanted to establish a bylaw that would protect certain historic buildings by placing them into a "special places" category. But Arlington did not want to rely on the specific statutes that might have given them the power to do so. It did not want to establish a separate historic district pursuant to its powers delegated by chapter 40C[32] because that would require establishing several districts, each of which would encompass only one building. For the same reason it did not want to establish special zones pursuant to its zoning powers under chapter 40A.[33] Although neither of these statutes expressly prevented the town from acting on its own in the manner it envisioned, fears that a court would hold that its bylaw frustrated these existing state statutes led the town to file a home rule petition seeking legislative authorization of its action rather than going ahead with confidence in its home rule authority. By offering an alternate, but safer, path, the ability to obtain enabling legislation from the state thus discourages municipalities from using their home rule authority.

One legal counsel for towns in the Boston area offered another example of the practice. He noted that towns routinely seek special legislative permission whenever they enter into a long-term lease because "there's some reference to time limits in the statutes," even though, in his view, most long-term leases would not be covered by those statutes. Some of the impetus for this caution, he and other respondents noted, may come from the private parties with whom the municipality is dealing. They may be fearful of entering into a loan agreement or a land deal with a municipality without complete assurance about the locality's authority—assurance that can best be secured through special state legislation.

The internalization of this kind of cautiousness structures the second category of municipal response to the grant of home rule power: communities come to believe that the grant of home rule authority in fact did not turn over any real power to them. To some extent, this sentiment is unwarranted as a legal matter. The legal counsel for two municipalities in the region explained that "there's still a great tendency on the part of municipalities to assume that they need legislative authority to do things that they probably have the right to do. [There is a] huge number of home rule petitions filed in the legislature, most of which are unnecessary." Nevertheless, the sense that localities lack legal authority clearly shapes how municipal officials conceive of their legal options. One town administrator told us that towns "do not have home rule powers, the state controls everything that we do." Another felt that municipalities have home rule in name only. From his own experience and his comparison with other home rule states, he found the traditional concept of home rule flipped in Massachusetts: "If it doesn't specifically say that you can do it, you can't." A third echoed the sentiment by saying: "We interpret [the list of what municipalities can do] as being exhaustive, and we don't do things that aren't on the list." A respondent from Holliston summed up this attitude: "Home Rule is very limited in Massachusetts; the laws define what local governments can and can't do, not like in other states . . . where local power is the default. In Massachusetts, the state sets the rules and guidelines; it's a very controlled atmosphere."

It is important to note that a number of respondents had the opposite view of local home rule authority. They described their home rule experience according to its traditional definition—as a municipality's power to act whenever the state has not specifically prohibited it from doing so. However, the frequency of this answer was low—even among the majority of respondents who concluded that home rule was, as an overall matter, strong in the state. The officials that expressed this more positive view of their home rule powers seemed confident that the general grant of home rule authority enabled them to proceed as they saw fit. For example, an official from Bedford noted that, even though there are instances where the state intruded, for the most part a town could proceed "without worrying about what the state says." A respondent from Littleton stated that home rule was very important because it allowed the town to adopt bylaws, and not just zoning bylaws, to address specific problems rather than relying on the state. An official from Boxborough agreed, calling the authority to adopt by-laws part of what "allows us to avoid a cookie-cutter approach to problems." An administrator from Nahant further supported municipal independence by stating: "We don't usually go to the state for anything." According to him, Nahant's town meetings and its home rule powers are capable of handling most local issues. As a town official from Hamilton explained: "We have found the basic structure of local government created by the underlying provisions of the Massachusetts General Laws to work well without frequent forays to the legislature to seek additional power. It may be that our Board of Selectmen interprets things so that they can solve local problems with the power they have."

Some of the municipalities that felt they were able to act independently of state supervision said so, however, not out of confidence in their home rule authority but almost in defiance of state power. One municipal administrator, who wished to remain anonymous, stated that he was able to accomplish all of his municipal objectives not by invoking home rule authority but by taking no notice of potential state interference. Another said that most of the time they "ignore the state and try to maximize the interest of the community." It is, then, not the home rule authority that instills these officials with the feeling that they can act. On most issues, they feel the state will never check and never know.

HOME RULE PETITION AUTHORITY

One of the traditional reasons given for granting home rule power is to reduce local lawmaking by the state legislature. Perhaps because the general grant of home rule power is perceived to be so narrow, however, the home rule petition process—the process by which individual localities may petition the state for legislation affecting only their locality—was for a large number of respondents the essence of home rule in Massachusetts. As a city official from Medford put it, in the absence of some express state statutory authority: "You don't have a lot of ways to go without petitions." It is important to recognize that the term "home rule" has a very different meaning in the home rule petition process than it does for the general grant of home rule authority. The general grant of home rule authority is designed to allow a municipality to make a decision on its own. The home rule petition process, by contrast, is designed to empower the state legislature to authorize a municipality to act. The home rule petition process, in other words, is not a way of empowering the locality to determine its policies. It puts the critical decision making power in the hands of the state.

Indeed, the home rule petition process, established by section 8 of the Home Rule Amendment, empowers the state to act in a way it could not otherwise act. The state is not generally allowed to pass legislation that governs only one locality.[34] Even when the legislature tries to pass a law that affects a general category of municipalities, the state action may be considered unlawful if the category actually consists of only one locality.[35] This ban on special legislation is intended to preserve local control by protecting cities from unwanted state legislative interference in local affairs. The home rule petition process grants an exception to this prohibition if the special legislation meets certain conditions. One of these conditions is that the locality must file a home rule petition asking for the special legislation from the state. The idea behind this exception is that, because the special state legislation is requested by the locality, it is likely to take the form of a delegation of power to the locality rather than an unwanted intrusion into local concerns.

Under the home rule petition process, then, the locality seeks out the special legislation, but the power the municipality exercises, if the petition is granted, comes from the state. If the state denies the petition, the municipality has no power to act. Equally importantly, the locality only obtains the power to act in the precise manner set forth in the special legislation. Any deviation from the precise terms would require the locality to return to the legislature for new special legislation—unless they were willing to assert independent home rule authority pursuant to the general grant of power the Home Rule Amendment confers. Of course, were they to follow that route, they would run the risk that the original special legislation might be deemed to preempt such an assertion of the home rule power.

The Importance of the Home Rule Petition Process

In practice, reliance on the home rule petition process is extensive. Because it applies only to one locality, this kind of legislation is called "special legislation." But there is nothing special about it. Quite the contrary. Special legislation consistently makes up more than 50 percent of all laws passed by the state each year. Many more petitions are filed that do not become law. Almost every municipality we interviewed reported having filed a home rule petition in recent years. For many municipalities in the Boston region, the home rule petition is the central focus of their exercise of their home rule power and the primary, if not the only, avenue for some form of local empowerment apart from more general state legislative authorizations. In the municipalities that believed that there is no genuine grant of home rule authority, the home rule petition is treated as the basic tool of empowerment for local initiatives. As an official from Franklin put it: "We can't do anything outside the laws of the Commonwealth . . . without their permission. That's why there's a zillion home rule petitions all the time." In municipalities that believed that they had the ability to act when no express state preemption exists, the home rule petition frequently is relied on as a guarantee that their legal authority will not be subject to challenge. An official from Everett explained: "Even if there is the slightest gray area, we do go through the home rule petition process."

Reflecting the importance of the home rule petition process to localities, numerous municipal officials in our interviews, when asked about home rule, immediately identified the term "home rule" with the petition process. These officials understood home rule as providing a direct avenue through which localities can apply for state laws that empower a specific city or town. The widespread identification of "home rule" with the home rule petition process is both ironic and troubling. It is ironic because, even prior to the Home Rule Amendment, localities had the right to seek authorizing legislation from the state legislature. The state constitutional grant of home rule did not confer this power. It is troubling because it testifies to the sentiment expressed by so many of the officials we interviewed that the general grant of the home rule power conferred by the Home Rule Amendment offers much less than it might seem. The home rule petition process is so central, it appears, because many municipal officials believe there are few alternative routes to securing local power tailored to their needs.

Because the home rule petition is the centerpiece of the Home Rule Amendment for most of the municipalities we interviewed, it is also the part of the Home Rule Amendment that invoked the widest range of reactions. This difference of opinion results from distinctive qualities of the petition process itself. For some, the process seems so easy that it has become an integral and conventional part of municipal governance. Officials from Medway, Everett and Arlington noted that their town had never had a problem getting a petition granted. An Arlington official said that the town regularly files a petition to ensure that they have the appropriate legal authority to undertake local initiatives. A respondent from Malden even joked by saying that, with all the petitions the city was filing, it felt like the state legislature was working for them. For many localities, the home rule petition process is thus perceived less as an indication of the state's control over their activities than as a routine procedure for conducting their business. To quote an official from Westwood, the process is "a way of getting the issue on the table at the state level—to get a homegrown idea into the state legislature."

Complaints About the Home Rule Petition Process

Important as the home rule petition process is to many municipalities, many of the officials we spoke with described it as anything but a sure thing or a useful source of local empowerment. A clear majority of respondents reported that home rule petitions are not always granted. Many of the town and city officials with whom we spoke stated that the process is so difficult that they have often modified their intended course of conduct or dropped their plans altogether in order to avoid having to go through it. In line with these sentiments, a number of officials we surveyed were quick to point to particularly frustrating episodes. An official from Acton told us how the town had wanted to change the way that it borrowed money to take advantage of falling interest rates. Doubtful that it possessed the home rule authority to make such a change—both because Section 7 of the Home Rule Amendment excludes borrowing from the general grant of home rule authority and because such a change might be preempted by state statutes—the town sought a home rule petition. "The [Joint] Committee loved our idea and said they weren't going to grant our town-specific petition because they wanted to change the rules for all towns! But guess what happened after that? They never changed the rule . . . ." An official from Concord reported a similarly frustrating experience. "We proposed a simple [land] swap . . . [to] get some land next to the pond so we could build a water treatment facility. Unfortunately, state law says the legislature must approve transactions dealing with the water supply. So we had to submit a petition for the swap. Would you believe that the legislature still hasn't approved it after eight years? Even though both parties agree that it's a good deal."

Given the risk that, as an official from Carlisle put it, petitions "will get put on the back burner because they don't rank very high in [the legislature's] over-all priorities," municipalities must rely heavily on their state representatives to push their particular petition through. It is not enough that the locality has approved the petition. Without a representative on the floor supporting the peti-tion, petitions often expire without any action being taken. Gaining the support of the state representative elected to represent residents in the locality is often more difficult than one might think. An official from Concord complained that state representatives do not fight for requests coming out of their home areas because they fear political reprisal or because political priorities on the state level deviate from what is requested on the local level. Some municipalities that file many home rule petitions (Malden being one) pointed out that state representa-tives can be frustrated when they are asked to advocate too many home rule peti-tions. State representatives are required to expend significant effort to get a petition out of a committee and passed by the state legislature. This effort can strain their resources. The nature of the relationship between the locality and the state representative can also affect the efforts of local home rule petitions. Some municipal officials reported having a difficult time getting petitions passed because of grudges between their representative and other representatives. Bypassing these political roadblocks requires energy and imagination.

Even if the local representative supports the petition, it may attract opposition from other legislators. One suburban town that wanted to establish a revolving loan fund to subsidize affordable housing—and feared that it lacked authority to do so—sought a home rule petition to secure the necessary power. The official we interviewed said that the "this petition has been tied up in committee for over a year because a legislator thinks that it's a backdoor attempt to avoid Proposition 2 1/2." Other local administrators expressed similar frustration with what they characterized as the influence of special interest lobbying on the state legislature. They pointed out that controversial local ordinances and bylaws, such as affordable housing initiatives and municipal employment law modifications, often attract strong challenges from private interest organizations. These challenges make a local petition politically charged and, thereby, dissuade state representatives from even addressing it. They also force localities to allocate time and resources to engage in their own lobbying efforts in order to get the state legislature to act on their petition. Municipalities without the endurance or desire to embroil themselves in such a political fight often just stay away from controversial initiatives in the first place.

There is another problem as well. Home rule petitions sometimes encounter potential difficulties at the state level not because of the substance of the particular petition but because granting it might generate a "slippery slope" of undesirable future consequences. Some respondents stated that the legislature is wary of granting petitions on issues that the state guards closely, such as revenue and finance, due to fears that granting them would encourage other municipalities to ask for the same. State and local officials are also guarded about petitions that might threaten legal or political challenges to the status quo. An official from Boxborough mentioned that, because home rule petitions often seek to address unfairness in the status quo, they draw attention to that unfairness. Drawing attention to these issues, however, could mean potentially expensive lawsuits. Therefore municipal and state governments may steer clear of certain kinds of petitions for fear of exposing the unfairness of the status quo, even when it means preserving that unfairness.

Procedural customs, most of which, while not required by statute, have become standard practice, also shape the home rule petition process. Respondents reported that the state legislature usually will not consider a petition if the membership of the municipal legislature and the state legislature changes between the time the petition was filed and the time the petition is being voted on. If the composition of the state legislature or municipal legislature changes, the petition is usually considered no longer viable. The locality therefore needs to refile the petition. This means, for many localities, that there is only a small window of time when petitions can be submitted for consideration before the next local election. Moreover, although the Home Rule Amendment does not require anything like local unanimity to put forth a petition, a number of respondents stated that the state legislature was unlikely to approve petitions if there was evidence of a substantial minority within the locality that was opposed to it. "If there is a sizeable opposition—say from a neighborhood group—they make an end-run and brow beat the legislature not to pass it," a town attorney reported. "This happened to us with a wireless telecommunications plan. We wanted to relocate an easement, but the opposition lobbied against it and we eventually withdrew."

As this last example illustrates, municipal efforts to support a petition do not end after the home rule petition is filed. The locality often needs to assume the role of active lobbyist in order to encourage the state to consider the petition and to combat opposition that may arise. This practice of post-petition lobbying by municipalities has become such a common tradition that, according to local officials we spoke with, many state officials will assume that the locality does not truly support a petition if it is not constantly followed up. As a result, even the kinds of petitions that are rarely denied may expire in the state legislature without any action being taken on them.

Finally, many petitions are granted on the condition that the proposed action also be authorized by a local referendum.[36] This requirement delays the desired results of the petition. Some localities complained that, with the petition process and the necessary referendum, it can take up to three years before a proposal actually becomes approved. Such a delay complicates large development projects involving private developers, especially those projects that require multiple petitions.

From the perspective of many municipalities, most of the difficulties that plague the home rule petition process are the consequence of actions of other interested parties or the state legislature. The difficulties are perceived to be such an integral part of the process that it makes them cautious about submitting a petition. As an official from Boxborough put it, the petition process can be "intimidat[ing]." Or, as another explained: "It's a god awful process." As a result, municipal officials sometimes use their understanding of the hazards of the process to reject potentially problematic local petitions before they are considered by the municipality, much less proposed to the state. In the City of Boston, which operates under a generous and powerful special act charter, the mayor sometimes uses his veto power to reject problematic proposals that originate from the city council when he feels that they will not be approved by the state if the city goes forward with the petition. An administrator from Cambridge similarly explained that the city would attempt to determine whether its petition would have any chance of succeeding before pursuing it: "In every home rule petition, the Council considers the likelihood of passage—just the real politics of the situation. . . . You do not want to be sending up petitions just to have them fail."

This hesitation to use the process has been ingrained into the system. At the same time, municipalities have internalized the home rule petition as an insurance policy, something they rely on whether they need it or not. Arlington is only one of the many towns that have decided to secure special legislation from the state with a petition instead of risking the possibility of being overturned. In this respect, the home rule petition process may be leading many municipalities to rely too much on the state legislature as opposed to their own independent powers of home rule, even as it fails to provide a ready means of empowering localities to do things that the general grant of home rule power fails to authorize them to do.

HOME RULE IDEOLOGY

Many of the municipal officials to whom we spoke referred to home rule not in terms of the technical ingredients of the Home Rule Amendment—the home rule charter authority, the general grant of home rule authority, and the home rule petition authority—but as an ideological position connected to community identity and self-determination. A Lincoln official said that "home rule power allows the town to pursue its particular vision." Another town official stated that "implicit in home rule is [a] local community's character and identity." A spokesman from Pembroke talked about the sense of community that home rule brings: "When you have home rule, it gives the community a sense of ownership . . . that they control things within their own community." An official from Gloucester echoed this sentiment. Although he began his answer admitting that he did not know what home rule really meant, he went on to say that if home rule meant internal accountability and having a community "stake in shaping [its] future," then home rule is important. For these localities, the ideology associated with home rule in the state is just as important, if not more important, than the actual legal powers that home rule provides.

Indeed, this sentiment seemed to underlie the responses of a number of local officials who did not identify the general grant of home rule authority as being of great importance but nonetheless regarded home rule as strong in Massachusetts. The ideological conception of home rule has an existence detached from the actual legal manifestation of home rule supported by the Home Rule Amendment. Very often municipalities that praised and defended home rule as an ideological belief were the very ones that were critical of the Home Rule Amendment for not giving municipalities any home rule. A respondent from Peabody stated that he was for home rule and defined it as the cities' right to determine their own destiny. Yet he was highly critical of the home rule structure, saying that there was only home rule up to a point because "big brother [the state] is always looking over [their] shoulders." An official from Milton expressed similar sentiments. He felt that municipalities had home rule in name only—that he had to ask the state for permission to do anything. Nonetheless, he proclaimed that municipalities would resist regionalism because "no town would want to give up their own sovereignty." He thus combined references to "sovereignty" with a belief that the town had no inherent authority to do anything without permission. Some municipal officials put the matter somewhat differently. They said that their constituents believed in home rule—that is, that they can control their own destinies—but that the truth was that they did not know how home rule worked. Their strong ideological faith in home rule was premised on a mistaken understanding of the powers that home rule provided cities and towns. As an official from Milford put it: "Do we have strong home rule? No, I don't think so! Whoever says we're particularly strong, I don't think they understand the concept."

Some respondents who emphasized the strength of home rule ideology in Massachusetts linked it to a pre-Revolutionary War sensibility that they associated with the Bay State. Explaining that "there's a strong spirit of self-determination" among the state's localities and that "they think of themselves as sovereign communities," a respondent from Littleton concluded that this sensibility "dates back to colonial times." A spokesman from Acton similarly noted a "fierce belief that you should be self-contained." He then asked, "Why is there this belief in self-containment?" The answer, he suggested, was that "it comes from the history of how towns used to form in Massachusetts. It used to be that as soon as you could afford your own church and preacher, you became a town. Well, that history created a huge emphasis on self-reliance." As an official from Ashland put it, home rule "is ingrained from how we started, the towns meetings of the Pilgrims." Interestingly, one official we spoke with conceived of the state's history quite differently. Arguing that in practice "towns need permission to do anything" and that "they lack the freedom to operate within broad parameters," an official from Holliston concluded that this situation was "consistent with a different philosophy that's prevalent in New England—that the state should keep an eye on local government and prevent too rapid change. The town meeting tradition was the backdrop of the state having the final say-so."

The ideological impressions of home rule's importance were not entirely positive though they were strongly felt. Municipalities sometimes complained about the parochial attitude that the ideology of home rule fosters. A Wakefield official commented on the hostility and suspicion towards one another caused by home rule parochialism. A Concord official similarly noted the "parochial outlook" resulting from a strong ideological home rule tradition. And another group of municipalities claimed that the lack of actual home rule power undermined the idea that Massachusetts had a strong home rule tradition even in the ideological sense.

These seemingly dichotomous views of home rule—in which municipal officials perceive it to be non-existent yet fundamental, important but problematic—are not necessarily contradictory. Instead, they reveal the complexity of home rule in the Boston region. Beneath the features of the Home Rule Amendment lies an alternate ideological image of home rule that mirrors the Amendment but has a life of its own. To examine what home rule in all its complexity means, we turn from the general provisions of state law that purport to secure home rule to an examination of specific areas of municipal and regional concern. In this way, we can begin to see home rule in action and to get a feel for the kinds of powers that local officials believe they possess and those they believe the state prevents them from asserting. Home rule, in all its various forms, is inscribed in a complex web of state statutes, legal regulations, historical traditions, and public expectations. One can understand the true breadth of state-imposed limitations on home rule only by examining how the powers conferred by the Home Rule Amendment operate in conjunction with these other ingredients of the legal structure. The next three chapters investigate this framework for municipal governance by discussing three traditionally established aspects of municipal governance: revenue and expenditures, land use, and education. This list is not designed to be exhaustive. Our interviews revealed, however, that municipal concerns regarding home rule consistently related to these three issues. In the last section of this report—where we discuss the relationship between home rule and regionalism in the Boston metropolitan area—we will return to the puzzle presented by the combination of ideological belief in home rule's existence, the recognition of the limits of municipal power, and the concerns about parochialism.

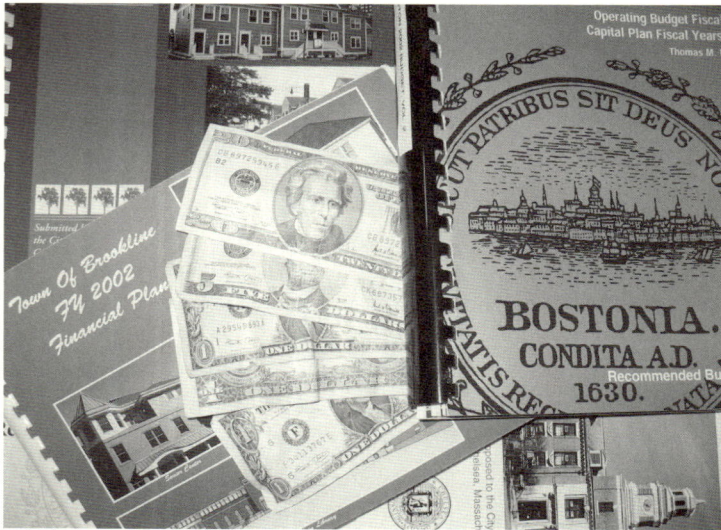

2. Home Rule in Action: Revenue and Expenditures

"The most important use [of home rule power] is finance authority, which is the area where we are most restricted."

—Public official from Medfield

Before a locality can take any action at all, it has to consider whether it has the financial resources to do so. A municipality's fiscal capacity is the cornerstone of its power: it establishes the extent of its ability to provide or expand services for its residents and its ability to react to regional economic changes. It is no surprise, then, that almost all of the municipal officials that we interviewed said that the budget was not only their primary responsibility but also their biggest problem. Several of these officials treated their municipality's lack of resources as a problem independent of the limitations on their home rule power. They argued that the problem with home rule in Massachusetts was one of a lack of resources rather than a lack of power. But, as other municipal officials recognized, much of a locality's ability to raise and allocate financial resources is governed by the limitations imposed by the Home Rule Amendment, along with a number of important state statutes.

Few respondents believed they had home rule in the sense of local fiscal control. Section 7 of the Home Rule Amendment and state laws regulating local taxation—including Proposition 2½—severely limit municipal revenue raising. At the same time, state statutes imposing unfunded mandates—as well as state statutes that authorize expenditures for some but not other purposes—undermine a city or town's ability to allocate whatever revenue it has. Working together, these aspects of the legal structure do more than simply restrict a municipality's control over its revenue and expenditures. As many of the officials we spoke with noted, they prevent there being any connection between a locality's ability to raise revenue and its ability to control expenditures.

REVENUE

As a legal matter, there is virtually no local home rule authority in Massachusetts over the raising of revenue. Section 7 of the Home Rule Amendment makes this point explicitly: "Nothing in . . . [the Home Rule Amendment] shall be deemed to grant any city or town the power . . . (2) to levy, assess and collect taxes; [or] (3) to borrow money or pledge the credit of the city or town." The powers to tax and borrow that municipalities do have are wholly a function of specific grants of authority from the state. In granting this authority, the state has not conferred broad local discretion. The state's control extends from the general to the particular—from the ability to establish general tax policy to day-to-day administrative supervision and review. It approves almost every revenue-related action a municipality takes. The state determines the limit on local property tax increases and the extent to which a municipality can borrow money. Although state law does confer some home rule power to charge fees, this local power is also limited in numerous ways, not the least of which is the possibility that a state court will characterize a local fee as an impermissible local tax. With access to locally generated revenue constrained, state aid comprises an increasingly significant portion of the revenue side of the local budget. State grants are a significant source of revenue, but they often come with strings attached. The infusion of state aid, therefore, does not suffice to secure fiscal home rule in the eyes of many of those officials we interviewed.

Against this background, a spokesman from Ashland said that, with respect to revenues, "generally speaking, the state is like Big Brother, overshadowing the towns, making sure they do everything the way they're supposed to, right or wrong." Given this understanding, a town official from Medfield spoke for many we interviewed when he argued that the most important thing that could be done to strengthen home rule in the state would be to provide some flexibility over taxation, "which is completely off limits." Or, as a city official from Salem explained: unless the legislature gives authority to raise revenue in a different way, "home rule becomes something that allows you to take care of a specific or minor problem, but not major issues."

Taxation and Proposition 2½

Because the Massachusetts Constitution, unlike that of some other home rule states, expressly denies cities and towns the ability to decide how to tax their own residents, local tax authority must come from the state. In Massachusetts, state law requires localities to rely on property taxes—rather than on income or sales taxes—for almost all of their locally generated tax revenue.[1] Because the majority of the cities and towns in the Boston area do not have a substantial amount of commercial or industrial development, this means they must obtain most of their tax revenue from property taxes on residential property. This unbalanced reliance on residential property taxes has led many local officials to institute programs—and to use their control over land use policy—to attract commercial and industrial development to diversify their tax base. Even if municipalities succeed in attracting new development, however, their ability to tax it is subject to the same state-imposed restrictions as are imposed on their ability to tax current residential property owners. The state strictly limits the amount of revenue cities and towns can derive from local property taxes—whether commercial, industrial, or residential. Their ability to tax property is subject, most importantly, to Proposition 2½, which took effect in 1980 having been adopted by referendum.[2]

Proposition 2½ establishes two different restrictions on property tax collection: a "levy ceiling" and a "levy limit." The levy ceiling provides that a locality can never levy property taxes in excess of 2.5 percent of the total and fair cash value of all of its taxable property. The second restriction, called the levy limit, determines the maximum amount that a municipality can raise its property tax in any given year.[3] The levy limit can be overridden. But, except in special and limited circumstances,[4] Proposition 2½ requires that the override be adopted through a local referendum. Voters can approve three types of overrides: a general operating override (which cannot exceed the levy ceiling); a debt exclusion (which can exceed the levy ceiling but only during the life of the obligation); and a capital expenditure exclusion (which also can exceed the levy ceiling but can last only one year).[5]

A few officials we interviewed praised the limits on local taxing power imposed by Proposition 2½. A town official from Pembroke argued that the measure "prevents a community like ours from really going crazy and really putting a burden on taxpayers. It has forced the towns to work within their means." An official from Westwood concurred, saying that the measure forced municipalities to be "more efficient." These comments were in the distinct minority. More municipal officials complained about the limitations of Proposition 2½ than about any other state regulation.

The concerns that so many local officials expressed were no doubt related to the fact that our interviews occurred at a time when the state was discussing plans to cut state aid to cities and towns. Because Proposition 2½ limits localities' ability to react to economic changes by increasing their own revenue, it has made the amount of state aid they receive of critical importance. Municipalities attempt to anticipate the state funding they will receive when they formulate their budget, but the actual amount is determined by the state on a year-to-year basis. As a result, the state might provide less than the locality has already planned to spend. When this happens, towns and cities have trouble reacting in part because their powers to raise revenue are strictly limited by Proposition 2½. The town official we interviewed from Millis described the situation this way: "It's becoming more difficult to meet budget needs because of the lack of flexibility with raising revenue. We really feel the real estate downturn, and we have no way to respond to economic shocks." An official from Melrose, facing a severe revenue shortfall because of potential cuts in state funding, said that "when the economy goes south, as it has recently . . . we can't react quickly enough except for job cuts." A spokesman from Medway also pointed to job cuts as the only way to balance the budget if the state reduces local funding.

Other officials noted that, while Proposition 2½ limits a municipality's power to increase property taxes, it does nothing to reduce local reliance on property taxes. In combination with other state laws, the measure serves only to constrain local fiscal control. "The most important use [of home rule power] is finance authority," an official from Medfield argued, "which is the area where we are most restricted. In spite of [Proposition] 2½, we're two-thirds dependent on property taxes. [We have n]o ability to use anything other than a very regressive tax to support our functions . . . ." Some municipal officials also complained that the formula used in calculating the yearly levy limit does not adequately take into account changing economic conditions outside of a municipality's control. A town administrator from Nahant pointed out that "the cost of living rises faster than their ability to raise revenue." Nahant has had to apply for two overrides in order to maintain operations, both of which passed by a slim margin.

Although Proposition 2½ affects all municipalities in Massachusetts, they are not equally impaired by its limitations. A few municipalities have a property tax base large enough that they do not need to tax up to their levy limit. This greatly enhances their ability to react to economic downturns. The difference between the current tax base and the levy limit provides a reserve fund that they can tap into at will. Some localities have gone further and created a "rainy-day" fund to compensate for sudden drop-offs in revenue. It is important to recognize that this ability to prepare for unexpected losses in revenue derives largely from the tax base that already exists, rather than from anything a city or town can proactively accomplish through its home rule powers. For example, Everett can tax under its levy limit—and also put away a substantial stabilization fund that it can tap into—because, unlike most communities in the Boston area, it possesses a strong industrial and commercial tax base that includes District Gas, which by itself brings in $3 million yearly in property taxes. By contrast, in residential communities, local officials are forced to tax up to or beyond the levy limit to cover expenditures and often lack the excess revenue to create a "rainy-day" fund that commercial or industrial properties might generate. Even affluent residential towns like Weston have sought Proposition 2½ overrides in the last few years in order to maintain their operating budget.[6]

Local officials had very different reactions to the fact that, under Proposition 2½, the levy limit can be overridden by referendum. For many, the override is a critical and integral part of their yearly budgetary procedure. It provides a means of retaining local fiscal control. Many localities have requested several overrides in recent years and plan to ask for more in the future. The town of Acton, for example, used the "debt exclusion" override to pay back $100 million worth of loans used for school and library renovations. A town official from Lincoln, which hasn't hesitated to use the Proposition 2½ override, called the override the most significant way for the town to overcome the limitations on its power.

But the Proposition 2½ override is not without its complications and problems. The fact that the override can only be achieved by winning a majority of the electorate in a referendum shifts decision making power away from elected city and town officials. In the end, overrides are frequently voted down by the electorate.[7] As a town administrator from Boxborough noted, lack of public knowledge regarding the fiscal capacity of a town makes an override a hard sell in some communities. Often, officials told us, residents are concerned with only one aspect of local governance. They will vote to preserve the budget on one service, such as education, and then vote down overrides because they expect the local officials to make budget cuts on other services even though they are already operating on a minimum budget. As a result, many municipal administrators we interviewed no longer see the override as a viable option. Since the initiation of an override vote costs a significant amount of money, officials in localities where there is little chance of an override being passed sometimes decide not to waste the money necessary to put an override vote on the ballot. Even some of those who have successfully used the override said that asking voters, year after year, to override the legal limit for the property tax levy to balance their budget is a very inefficient way to run a government.

Other State Controls Over Revenue

Proposition 2½ is only one example, albeit an important one, of state control over local revenue raising. From assessment to collection to receipt, the administration of the property tax is strictly regulated by the state. As an official from Bedford put it, there is "micromanagerial oversight over the town's finances to make sure [we] don't screw anything up fiscally." Although the state delegates the act of assessing property values for property tax purposes to local boards of assessment, all reassessments must be submitted to the state Department of Revenue for approval before they go into effect.[8] The tax rate of a municipality also cannot be officially fixed until it has been approved by the state.[9] This means that localities cannot send out property tax bills to their residents until they have been signed off by the Department of Revenue.[10] The state's review process occasioned strong criticism. An official from Middleton stated: "It's absurd how lengthy the state approval process is when the town wants to changes its property tax rate. Somehow in Massachusetts cities and town can't be trusted through the home rule process to do that so the state struck their finger in every part of it."

The Department of Revenue also requires local boards of assessment to submit their evaluations according to a given schedule. But the amount of time the Department of Revenue needs to give the locality its approval varies. Because some municipalities are very dependent on the property tax, this extra level of state authorization restricts their ability to manage their resources. Like many others, the town of Concord relies on the property tax for more than 80 percent of its revenues, and, a town official stated, the Department of Revenue "really drags its feet on giving approval; and this means that [the town is] set back by months." This official argued that "the state should set up a new system under which towns that have demonstrated their competence should be allowed to act with more freedom."

Finally, the state in exercising strict control over local taxing power does more than limit the ability of municipalities to raise revenues. It also limits local control over tax policy. For example, state law limits the ability of cities and towns to create exemptions from tax liability that might promote local interests. One town official argued that, as a way of responding to downshifts in the regional economy, localities should be able to adjust commercial tax rates downwards to promote economic development—a power that they now lack. Other municipal officials emphasized their desire to give tax abatements to elderly residents who were being driven out of town by ever increasing property tax rates. "One thing that I would love to be able to do is to give elders tax breaks from local property taxes—but taxation is one of these things that is particularly hard to get local control over," an official from Hamilton said.[11] From this perspective, the state's control over local taxation deprives municipalities not only of revenue but also of critical policy tools they need to shape and protect the character of their community.

Fees

The dramatic limits that state law imposes on local taxing power do not extend to all forms of raising local revenue. Local governments have the power under the Home Rule Amendment to impose fees as long as they pertain to a local service, are administrative in nature, and are not preempted by state law. Several municipalities have used this power to add or increase local fees to supplement their income in response to revenue shortages. To be sure, the local power to use fees as revenues sources is far from unlimited. Many fees—such as those for motor vehicle and boat registration—are imposed directly by the state. The proceeds of these fees go to the localities from which they are collected, but the state controls their assessment and collection. Other fees are directly tied to the administration of specific services and for that reason they are not as useful a source of revenue as are taxes. Nahant's official reported that the municipality has moved several public services, such as trash, water, and sewer, to a fee-based system, but the amount of revenue these fees can generate is limited because the market value of these services is limited.

The state also sets some of the fees that can be charged by a locality. If they do, municipalities must petition the state for changes. The City of Boston has petitioned the state to increase the towing fee for vehicles parked in violation of local ordinances. The authorization for the fee originally passed as special legislation, and the authorizing legislation allowed Boston to charge only $12 for towing fees while the actual cost of towing has increased to $128. Boston has thus been losing money on every vehicle it towed. But it cannot remedy this problem by itself. Somerville has also petitioned for an increase to parking fines assessed in the city. A city administrator from Somerville explained that the structure of its parking authority and authorizing legislation compelled the city to petition the state for this increase instead of changing it on its own. A July 8, 2003 story in the Boston Globe describing proposed state legislation illustrates the level of detail involved in state control over local fees:

> Under the [proposed] bill, the statewide cap for a variety of parking viola-
> tions would be raised from $15 to $25, with the amount for violations not
> paid within 21 days rising from $20 to $35. Boston would be freed from a
> state law that caps towing fees in the city at $12 and would instead be
> allowed to charge the statewide rate of $75. The city would also benefit from
> the repeal of a 1946 law exempting many parking lots from property taxes,
> which would generate $2 million for Boston. In addition, the statewide auto
> lease and rental surcharge would be doubled from 30 cents a day to 60 cents
> a day, increasing by $109.50 the annual fees leasers must pay to the cities and
> towns they live in.[12]

Even if state law does not dictate the fee that a locality may charge, municipalities must be careful that the fees they impose are not later characterized by the courts as taxes. If they are, they will be invalidated for exceeding the limits on the general grant of home rule authority set forth in Section 7 of the Home Rule Amendment. The current judicial definition of fees and taxes therefore has important consequences for local power. Municipalities can seek "fees" from an individual for benefits provided to that individual, but they cannot, without state authorization, seek "taxes" from such an individual for the harm that his or her actions causes the municipality. Using this test, courts have struck down a town's attempt to charge developers a "fee" designed to compensate it for the impact that the development had on the town's school system.[13] The court found that the fee was actually a tax that the town did not have power to levy.

Several municipal officials we interviewed were aware that the state limited impact fees, and they singled out this aspect of state law as one of the areas where greater local revenue raising power could be conferred upon local governments. In arguing for this enhanced power, these officials noted that municipalities in other states have greater authority to impose these kinds of fees than the cities and towns of Massachusetts. Until such authority is granted, localities must rely on the home rule petition process. With the permission of the state, Medford has established a linkage program that requires new businesses to pay money to the town to offset the costs that the business has on town residents.

Confusion over the line between permissible administrative fees and impermissible municipal taxation has led some municipalities to alter their intended course of conduct. The town of Topsfield wanted to raise the admissions fee for the local town fair by $1 so it could cover added costs. But fears that the increase in the ticket price would be construed as an impermissible "tax" compelled the town to keep the ticket price the way it was.

State Aid

State-imposed limits on municipalities' ability to generate their own revenue have made them increasingly dependent on state aid. Most municipalities rely on state aid to balance their operating budgets and, in our interviews, many municipal administrators (from Hull, Bedford, and Malden, for example) applauded the state for sharing state resources with them. These officials stressed that state aid is a primary way in which the state has been helpful to cities and towns.

Given the fact that state aid is such a critical element of a municipality's budget, however, it is not clear whether state aid should be understood as a charitable donation from the state to localities or as a state mechanism that undermines local home rule authority. In fiscal year 2001, state aid made up an average of 28 percent of local revenue across the state.[14] In the Boston area, this figure varied from 57 percent (Chelsea) to 5 percent (Hamilton).[15] Over the past two decades, state aid has made up an increasingly significant part of municipalities' budgets. This has not been an accident. Figures reveal that this increased dependence resulted directly from the passage of Proposition 2½. State aid was increased by over 20 percent in 1982 to compensate for a 13 percent decrease in property tax receipts caused by Proposition 2½. Since then, the state increased financial assistance to municipalities in order to lessen reliance on the property tax.[16] By limiting a municipality's control over its own revenue, Proposition 2½ thus increased financial dependence on the state and, thereby, replaced local fiscal independence with local dependence on the power of the state.

Unlike many inter-local "revenue sharing" programs, state aid in Massachusetts invariably comes with strict requirements. As a respondent from Peabody put it, "anytime state . . . money is involved, there are strings attached." And, he added, certain problems are never addressed because local governments concentrate their efforts on doing those things necessary to make them eligible to receive state aid. Because the amount of money that a locality receives is based on the state programs they qualify for, some municipalities "may not be doing what [they] really need to, but what will bring the money in." The only way municipalities can tap into this source of funds is to jump through the hoops laid down by the state or lobby from the sidelines for direct aid for their own purposes. Most localities do both. Even though the grants do not directly mandate municipal action or usurp municipal authority, their indirect economic influence leads municipalities to adopt the priorities of the eligibility requirements at the expense of unique local concerns. Structuring programs to maximize state aid, the Peabody official warns, "usually costs [a town] more in the long run."

Reliance on state aid comes with the additional risk that the state may back out of arrangements previously made, leaving the municipalities to pick up the tab for programs initiated in part out of a desire to qualify for state support. The risk is particularly severe because it is difficult for a municipality to change programs fast enough to account for shifts in state funding priorities. Municipalities are often left to work out on their own how to make up for the deficit that the state causes by withdrawing state aid that they counted on. A town official from Cohasset mentioned a state promise to reimburse the town for school renovations. He said the state has since backed out of this program to the tune of $41 million dollars. Now Cohasset is seeking to get a debt exclusion override to Proposition 2½ to cover the bill. A town official from Norfolk talked about a program mandated by the state in the 1970s that awarded increased pay to police officers if they took liberal arts classes. The Norfolk official reported that the state promised to fund 50 percent of this program when it started. At the time of our interview, the official said that Norfolk had not received any funding for this program.

EXPENDITURES

Home rule is generally understood to give municipalities control over issues of local concern. It is difficult to determine exactly what constitute issues of local concern. But municipal expenditures would seem to be an example. Nothing in the Massachusetts Constitution limits municipal control over expenditures in the way that Section 7 of the Home Rule Amendment and Proposition 2½ limit the ability to raise revenue. Quite the contrary: Massachusetts has a state law that limits the state's ability to impose financial obligations upon localities. Yet almost all the municipal officials we interviewed were critical of the state's substantial control over their expenditures—control that ranges from state-imposed unfunded mandates to limits contained in state enabling legislation to rules that govern local public works projects. By establishing a legal structure that compels municipalities to channel resources to fund state priorities, state policy concerning local expenditures often resembles a form of local administration of state programs rather than a program for promoting local control. Many officials thought that local fiscal decision making on the spending side was as controlled by state priorities as municipal decision making on the revenue side.

The state's control over how localities may spend their own funds is not always obvious. State legislation authorizing local expenditures can itself limit a locality's ability to allocate funds. Consider, from this perspective, Chapter 40 of the Massachusetts General Laws, which contains a section entitled "purpose for which towns may appropriate money." Although this statute authorizes towns to spend money, the specificity of its provisions can be read not simply as empowering towns but as limiting their ability to appropriate and allocate resources for other purposes. Sections 5A and section 6, for example, enable a locality to appropriate money into a "reserve fund for extraordinary expenditures," and section 5B allows for the creation of a "stabilization fund." (No more than 3 percent of the preceding year's fiscal budget can go into a municipality's extraordinary expenditures fund, and no more than 10 percent can go to the stabilization fund.) The fact that these funds are defined narrowly for specific purposes would support an interpretation that the state intended this list of funds to be exhaustive. If so, any type of fund that does not fit one of the enumerated categories would require a petition to the state. A fund could not be established simply through the exercise of a municipality's home rule authority. It's not surprising, therefore, that when Franklin wanted to create a special fund to save the proceeds from a lawsuit it won, it filed a home rule petition to the state to secure the necessary authority.[17]

The most dramatic way in which the state regulates local expenditures is through unfunded mandates. Municipal officials affected by programs mandated by the state usually understand them to be worthy endeavors. But their implementation takes away a municipal government's power to decide where to allocate its limited resources. Localities seeking to balance their budgets are required to cut services that have local importance in order to adapt to the preferences of the state. Because so many state laws have this effect, many municipal officials identified unfunded mandates as a primary impediment to home rule. "State mandates significantly limit your discretion," according to a respondent from Saugus. "They widen the gap on how much is left over for other services." An official from Hamilton was even more critical: "If we have had problems with state officials it is because they are just enforcing the laws, and they forget the costs they impose locally. The unfunded mandate is our biggest complaint. We are left holding the bag."

In theory, unfunded state mandates should no longer be an issue for Massachusetts cities and towns. One of the elements of Proposition 2½ was a provision that no unfunded mandates could be imposed upon unwilling localities after 1981. More specifically, this part of Proposition 2½, often referred to as the "local mandate" provision, prevents the state from "imposing any direct service or cost obligation upon any city or town" without either local approval or full appropriation of state funds for the purpose of the mandate.[18] With this provision barring unfunded mandates in mind, one can understand Proposition 2½ as an attempt to embrace an intermediate position concerning local autonomy. While it restricted municipal collection of property taxes, it simultaneously promised to enhance local autonomy by restricting state intervention in, and control over, local affairs. Proposition 2½ may thus have initially been perceived, in part, as an effort to expand home rule power.

Yet Proposition 2½ is now remembered only as limiting municipal power, and unfunded state mandates are still a major concern for cities and towns in the Boston metropolitan area. There are two reasons for this. First of all, most of the unfunded mandates that adversely affect municipal budgets were imposed prior to 1981, and they were not affected by Proposition 2½'s prohibition of unfunded mandates. While Proposition 2½'s restrictions on municipal revenue were effective immediately, municipalities were not exempted from state mandates then in effect. Secondly, the state legislature has been able to find ways around the local mandate prohibition that do not violate it on its face. For example, Lexington and Newton prevailed in an unfunded-mandate lawsuit against the state, successfully defeating a statutory amendment that expanded the local obligation to provide private school transportation.[19] The state responded, however, by passing a second statute conditioning all state reimbursements for pre-1981 mandates on local acceptance of the challenged amendment. When the new statute was challenged by the same municipalities, the Supreme Judicial Court found that there was no violation of the prohibition. The court explained that "there is . . . nothing to prevent the Legislature from forcing the acceptance of [the private school transportation amendment] upon reluctant cities and towns by providing benefits it has no obligation to provide."[20]

Unfunded mandates come in many guises. State laws may attempt to ensure minimum levels of quality for some of the services that municipalities provide their residents. These quality standards are designed to maintain uniformity within the state for these services. Most of the required standards are imposed with little or no state funding, making it hard for a locality to adjust its current budget to come up to these standards. Alternatively, the state sometimes seeks to promote quality by directly mandating certain levels of local expenditures, as is the case with education. Numerous officials complained about the costs imposed by the Educational Reform Act, a state law that mandates a minimum educational spending level for every city and town in the state.[21] While recognizing the importance of education, many municipal administrators, like one from Salem, thought that the state should set guidelines and expectations but let localities decide how to meet them without requiring specific levels of spending. For many municipalities (such as Melrose and Hamilton), expenditures on education make up more than 50 percent of their total budget.[22] As a result, state mandates on educational spending limit their ability to control a significant percentage of their expenditures while increasing the pressure to raise revenues. According to an official from Nahant, the minimum mandated educational spending level is higher than the amount that Nahant is able to raise under Proposition 2½.

State law can also impose an unfunded mandate by compelling the provision of a service that otherwise might not be provided at all, let alone at the same level. The mandated service most often mentioned in our interviews was the state requirement that localities offer special education programs.[23] Local officials agreed that special education was important, but they pointed out that the program did not take into account the size, fiscal capacity, and needs of specific towns. A respondent from Swampscott noted that such a state mandate is particularly burdensome for small towns. The special education budget that the state sought to mandate, she pointed out, is larger than the entire operating budget for their high school. An official from Malden said that almost 30 percent of the city's $42 million school budget goes to special education programs. He recognized that there were many special education students in Malden and agreed that special education was a laudable goal, but he complained about the lack of state funding for the mandate. An official from Salem, facing similar financial problems, expressed a sentiment other municipal administrators echoed: "If these mandates or programs are worthy, the state should fund them." Possibly in response to this kind of criticism, the state legislature recently established a special education reimbursement program that offers additional state aid for "eligible instructional costs associated with implementing individual education plans, so-called, of students receiving special education services."[24] This program has been placed on indefinite hold, however, due to the state's current economic constraints.

Another example of a mandated service that municipal officials identified as restricting their budgetary control in significant ways was the state requirement to provide municipal employee health insurance. The state requires cities and towns to provide health insurance to their employees through a system approved by the state. As noted by municipal officials from Medford and Melrose, health insurance providers have increased premium costs by as much as 20 percent. For Medford, the official reported, the shortfall in state aid combined with the increases in health insurance expenses will cost an extra $6 million. Some municipalities (such as Holliston) have established regional health insurance programs to take advantage of group rates to offset this additional burden. Others (such as Wakefield) have not been able to establish such cooperative efforts. There is not much a municipality can do, other than these inter-local efforts, to protect itself from the cost increases charged by health insurance providers. An official from Everett explained that the state's rules concerning health insurance for municipal employees require every municipal union to agree to an increase in premiums. "There are roughly twenty-one unions in this city that I have to go to and say, 'I need some increases in these premiums.' We have unions for the clericals, laborers, school teachers. Any one retains veto power under state law. This really stifles communities that are faced with incredibly rising costs of health insurance." Yet, he added, it would be virtually impossible to get a home rule petition passed that would exempt the city from the provision.

Even when the state offers grants to pay for the mandates it imposes, the offer of funds can restrict and confine municipalities as well as assist them. A town official from Norfolk commented on the "professional development mandate" passed by the state. This mandate requires all schools to establish a training program for education-related employees within the public school system. Its purpose is to educate teachers about new developments in their field of study and to foster techniques in diverse teachings styles and collaboration among teachers.[25] The budget for this program is to come out of the educational budget for the individual schools, but it can be supplemented by state grants provided by the state Board of Education. Eligibility for this state assistance is conditioned on the amount of funding a municipality is willing to allocate to its schools. Any municipality that reduces the funding for public education from the previous fiscal year loses eligibility for state funding for professional development.[26] State assistance is also withdrawn if the municipality's absolute level of financial support for education declined in any year since 1986, adjusted for inflation. The professional assistance mandate thus does more than require expenditures to achieve state professional training objectives. The grants that support this mandate indirectly restrict municipalities' control over their overall educational budget. If the municipality decides to cut educational spending because of financial shortages or other priorities, state assistance for professional development is also reduced.

Finally, several officials criticized state regulations that control local public works projects as being, in effect, unfunded state mandates. Several officials pointed to the requirement that the police officer positioned at street construction projects be paid at a set wage, one that applies uniformly to all construction projects regardless of size or location.[27] As a result, the mandate disproportionately impacts small towns and minor construction projects. An official from Norfolk reported that the town recently buried utility wires on a seldom-used street. Although the total project budget was only $120,000, the mandated overtime salary for the police officer to direct traffic cost the city $33,000, more than 25 percent of the total project budget. The town official said that Norfolk decided to go ahead with the project anyway. But officials from other towns noted that mandates such as this discourage them from undertaking minor repairs or renovations because of the added overhead costs that would be required.

Other officials expressed concern about the costs imposed by the Massachusetts prevailing wage law, which establishes the minimum hourly wage that can be paid to employees working on government sponsored projects.[28] The wage law applies to specified individuals, such as contractors moving office furniture or working on the construction of public works. Whenever a municipality hires contractors for these purposes, it must pay the wage established by the state. An official from Walpole noted that the required wage is often 30–40 percent higher than the market rate in the private sector for the same type of work. As a result, this requirement significantly increased the cost of its municipal projects.

THE REVENUE–EXPENDITURES RELATIONSHIP

The conventional understanding of fiscal capacity for any organization imagines a close interdependence between revenue and expenditures. For most organizations, the level of expenditures is determined by assessing the needs of the organization, the costs of satisfying those needs, and the potential revenue available to pay for them. Unlike organizations that follow this conventional model, municipalities in the Boston area manage a much more complicated relationship between revenue and expenditures. As we have seen, numerous state statutes and regulations limit their ability to raise revenue. At the same time, a variety of state provisions make localities responsible for expenditures that they cannot avoid. Many municipal officials therefore do not see the budgeting process as enabling them independently to assess local needs, the costs of meeting them, and the means of paying for them. State limits on revenue raising and state commands to spend money combine to make the local assessment of needs a luxury that municipalities cannot afford. Even though it is generally understood that municipalities have control over their own budgets, that control in fact often requires them to cut programs and services not mandated by the state and to lobby the state for more aid, notwithstanding the strings that will be attached to it if it is obtained.

To get a feel for the disconnect between revenues and expenditures in the current structure, and thus the limits of local fiscal control, consider how actual budgeting practice compares to the description of the budgeting process set forth in a standard text on state and local taxation in Massachusetts. The text describes a process in which the municipality sets its tax rate after the municipal legislature approves an appropriation based on estimated local expenditures. Once the appropriation is established, anticipated state aid, fees, and other income from state funds are subtracted. The resulting figure is the amount that needs to be raised by taxation. This amount is then divided by the total property valuation, and the result determines the property tax rate. This procedure suggests that revenue is calculated from the level of expenditures that a locality needs to make. Fees and state aid are treated as supplements to the budget, not as critical component of it; they are subtracted out before the local tax rate is determined. For the most part, this model imagines a traditional interconnection between revenue and expenditures. One is calculated in terms of the other.[29]

This conventional model is not followed because of Proposition 2½, unfunded state mandates, and state limits on a locality's ability to find alternative sources of income to the property tax. Most municipalities do not decide how much they want to spend on services and then use that figure to calculate tax rates. Rather, they describe a situation in which revenues are predetermined due to state limits, a large portion of their expenditures are set by state mandates, and state aid—beyond their capacity to guarantee—is critical. For many municipalities, if local expenditures were calculated independent of revenue, the resulting tax rate would exceed the levy limit set by Proposition 2½. At the same time, unfunded state mandates establish an initial expenditure budget not locally chosen. State control over revenue and expenditures thus turns municipal budget calculations into an algebra equation that squeezes out local discretion. The only variables in the equation that municipal authorities can use to adjust revenue and expenditures are the local services and programs that are not controlled by state regulations. In the end, much of a municipality's actual power over its finances involves cutting these locally initiated programs. An official from Acton described the current budgetary situation this way: "[T]he strength of Acton is in its school system. The preponderance of new residents come here for the good schools. And the town spends over 70 percent of its revenues on the schools. Most similar towns are only around 50 percent, if that. As a consequence, we have relatively less money for services like roads, etc. Under Prop. 2½, we just can't make this money materialize."

This finance structure has not just left localities with less control over their budgets than is often imagined. This structure directly affects municipalities' capacity to control the character of their community. A town administrator from Reading discussed how the town's inability to control its revenue collection is part of a causal chain that exacerbates the town's problems because it increases expenditures without raising revenue. Without the ability to levy taxes or to find ways other ways to raise income, Reading instituted a property tax up to its levy limit. Attempts to override that limit failed the last two times they were tried. Yet because the property tax rate is now higher than in areas around it, and because Reading feels it is unable to make adjustments to that rate, Reading's elderly residents, impacted by the property tax, have moved out only to be replaced by families with kids. This increase in school-age children has led to an increase in educational services and in policing costs, which in turn has required more revenue to pay for these increased costs. Yet because the property tax is already levied at its maximum, and because the town lacks the tools to make its tax policy more accommodating to long-term elderly residents, the municipality can only react to these changes by cutting more services, trimming back on personnel, or, potentially, relying on its land use powers to limit new residents. In this way, the lack of local fiscal control makes it difficult for Reading to maintain the character of its community. Instead, fiscal concerns largely beyond its control shape the kind of community that the municipality becomes.

3. Home Rule in Action: Land Use

"If home rule authority . . . really existed, [then] cities and towns wouldn't have to go through the charade of asking for a Community Preservation Act and then subsequently not adopting it. In my view, it's a failure."

—Public official from Middleton

The powers and political concerns of the cities and towns in Massachusetts are defined in terms of the ability to administer and regulate a specific area of land—a subdivision of the state. A municipality's boundaries define its legal jurisdiction, and the appeal of home rule focuses the community's attention on issues within those boundaries. An examination of the legal structure that empowers or restricts a locality's control over the physical manifestation of its "home" is, therefore, critical to an understanding of the extent of home rule that municipalities in the region possess.

Municipal power to regulate the use of land within local borders derives primarily from state statutes rather than the grant of home rule authority. Many officials nonetheless identified their land use powers as broad and important, and they specifically commented on the significance of their power to zone, a power largely controlled by a state statute known as Chapter 40A. A respondent from Concord pointed out that, even though zoning bylaws, like any other town bylaws, require the approval of the Attorney General, they have generally been approved with little trouble. Others noted that there is a wide range of land use by-laws and ordinances in the region, ranging from those permitting cluster developments (Lexington) to those preserving open space (Hopkinton) to those providing for planned residential conservation communities (Acton). A town official from Boxborough told us that the town has used its delegated land use powers to adopt strict protections for wetlands.

The municipal land use power is, however, more limited than that of the state. Unlike the broad constitutional grant of authority given the state, municipal land use power is restricted by the terms of the relevant state statutes. Not surprisingly, therefore, some officials painted a more mixed assessment of their land use powers. They portrayed their land use power as driven less by local planning judgments than by the fiscal pressures that they attributed to state control of their revenues and expenditures. Several officials commented that these external influences led them to pursue land use policies that reduced the number of children moving into their communities, given the educational costs they bring. Others said that concerns about state preemption led them to shy away from strict environmental regulations that would preserve natural resources within municipal boundaries. Still others raised concerns about the scope of their legal power to regulate subdivisions or control growth. As an official from Medfield put it: "The only way to preserve open space is to acquire the property. There is no other way. Because of Massachusetts' recognition of property rights, municipalities and the state are restricted in what they can do." An official from Holliston even complained that the required Attorney General approval of by-laws made it difficult for towns to manage growth if they maintained the town meeting form of government. "To control sprawl . . . you need town meeting action, which can take time," the official explained. "If we had more latitude from the state it would be faster. For example, we could allow town officials more latitude with zoning bylaws or shorten the time for state review."

To provide a sense of the kind of authority municipalities have over land use policy, we discuss below three basic ingredients of the local land use power: the Zoning Act, which delegates the zoning power to localities; the Regional Planning Law, which mandates the accommodation of affordable housing devel-opments; and the Community Preservation Act, which provides municipalities with financial resources to buy, develop, and allocate local property. A focus on these statutes will demonstrate that state law does more than simply empower localities to control the land within their boundaries. It also places significant limits on the independent local autonomy often associated with the term "home rule." The Zoning Act authorizes local action, but it contains restrictions on the exercise of municipal power. The Regional Planning Law not only mandates the accommodation of affordable housing, but it does so without empowering local-ities to construct affordable housing on their own terms or enabling them to pre-serve affordable housing once it has been built. The Community Preservation Act empowers localities to raise money to protect and develop local property, but it has been criticized for internal inconsistencies and allocational inequalities that make it less than a simple grant of additional local authority.

ZONING

Zoning power in Massachusetts derives from the state constitution. Article 60 of the state constitution grants to the state legislature the power to "to limit build-ings according to their use or construction to specified districts of cities and towns." By enacting the Zoning Act—Chapter 40A of the General Laws—the state has delegated its zoning power to the state's municipalities. Chapter 40A gives municipalities significant control over local zoning issues. The courts have reinforced the extent of this local power through broad interpretations of Chapter 40A. By focusing on the intended purpose of the legislation rather than on specific grants of power, they have given substantial deference to municipal zoning regulations when challenged by private parties. Many officials mentioned the power to zone as one of the most significant aspects of their local authority. To be sure, this power, as many of those we interviewed noted, has been an obstacle to inter-local cooperation. Nevertheless, as a Bedford official observed, "towns feel they have gained some power over their own zoning and they don't want to give it up to anyone."

Characterization of Land Use Ordinances and Bylaws

Municipal regulations regarding land use usually take the form of zoning ordinances and by-laws. Before the passage of the Home Rule Amendment, the status of these ordinances and by-laws was relatively clear: municipal zoning was an exercise of the state power delegated to localities by Chapter 40A. As a result, any exercise of that power had to conform to the requirements outlined in Chapter 40A. There was no other source of authority. After the passage of the Home Rule Amendment, the legal foundation of a municipality's powers over land use has become potentially broader. The Massachusetts Supreme Judicial Court has recognized land use regulations to be a part of a municipality's general home rule authority, an authority that does not depend on power being specifically delegated by the state. It identified zoning regulations as "one of a city's or town's independent municipal powers included in article 89, section 6's [the Home Rule Amendment's] broad grant of powers to adopt ordinances or by-laws for the protection of the public health, safety, and general welfare."[1]

The court also noted, however, that a limitation in Section 6 of the Home Rule Amendment requires that the exercise of a municipality's home rule powers conform to state statutes.[2] As a result, Chapter 40A regulates a municipality's ability to pass land use regulations whenever the regulation is classified as a zoning ordinance or bylaw. The determination whether a specific by-law or ordinance is a "zoning regulation," subject to the procedural requirements and limitations of Chapter 40A, or a general exercise of a locality's police powers, authorized by the Home Rule Amendment, is therefore important. Unfortunately, the judicial interpretation of the line between the two has generated considerable uncertainty.[3] This uncertainty—coupled with the concern that the state's zoning enabling act occupies the field of land use policy and thus ousts seemingly complementary local authority—has led many municipalities to exercise caution by not relying on their home rule authority. Most municipalities stick with the requirements and restrictions of Chapter 40A. Some municipalities, such as Arlington, do not want to be restricted by the state act, but they prudently file a home rule petition to avoid the costly possibility that regulations will be challenged in court if they rely on their general home rule power as the justification for the enactment. The result is that land use power generally tends to be governed by the terms of Chapter 40A, although other measures, such as the Massachusetts Subdivision Control Law,[4] are also significant.

Frustration of Land Use Planning Efforts

Chapter 40A and related statutes do not simply ensure that the exercise of local land use power will be upheld if challenged in court. As several respondents pointed out, they also play a substantial role in frustrating local land use planning. Indeed, the American Planning Association recently listed Massachusetts as one of the states with the most outdated land use laws, and the Zoning Reform Working Group of its local chapter concluded: "Although technically a 'home-rule' state, the statutes that govern planning and land use regulation are so restrictive to local authority as to make home rule more an illusion than a reality in Massachusetts."[5] The limitations manifest themselves in a variety of ways, from prohibitions in Chapter 40A against localities establishing maximum floor areas for houses[6] (which communities might use to prohibit so-called McMansions) to provisions of the Subdivision Control Law (which insulate from local review all subdivisions fronting existing roads).[7] We consider here, as examples, a few of the substantial limitations that Chapter 40A places on effective local land use planning.

One of the key obstacles that Chapter 40A presents is that it exempts certain land uses from local zoning. There are many such exemptions—dealing, for example, with the use of land for religious or educational purposes, child care facilities, the use of building materials, and the use of antennas (unless, that is, these regulations meet specified statutory exceptions).[8] In addition, state property and that of its assignees is exempted from local zoning laws.[9] This exemption for state property extends to the use of land by private entities as long as they are being employed by the state.[10] In fact, state departments can grant exemptions to these private entities without considering alternatives, and the exemptions are usually decided through a narrow site-specific analysis. The site need not be the most ideal site in the municipality. Nor does it matter that there may be an alternative that can better satisfy the demands of all the parties involved. Thus the Department of Public Utilities, not the municipality, has the final authority to regulate the placement of transmission lines.[11] And it can exempt utility companies from zoning restrictions without considering alternate sites proposed by the locality.[12]

These exemptions undermine local efforts to create a master plan. Massachusetts cities and towns are required to prepare such a master plan, although no statutory provision makes such a plan enforceable in state court. Yet even if such a plan were accorded legal significance by the state, state statutory exemptions would ensure that the state agencies considering overrides of community zoning decisions would not have to conform to it. To be sure, Executive Order 385, issued by Governor Weld, requires "[a]ll agencies [to] promote, assist and discharge their duties with full consideration of local or regional growth management plans that have been formally accepted by the affected municipalities."[13]

But this executive order simply requires "consideration" of local plans and applies only if a locality actually adopts a growth plan. The lack of a more powerful consistency requirement between a master plan and what is being implemented, whether by the locality or the state, has led one critic to wonder, "Why plan at all?"[14]

Other aspects of Chapter 40A frustrate local planning by limiting a municipality's authority to change existing zoning. In recent years, state agencies and activists concerned with neighborhood design have criticized the usual pattern of zoning in the state's towns and cities for promoting cookie-cutter style, conventional residential development. Some have even argued that current local zoning codes prevent fast-growing suburbs from acquiring the look and feel of the traditional New England towns that constitute one of the region's greatest assets. Many towns have therefore begun to re-evaluate their zoning codes, and some of the officials we interviewed made positive references to their ability to experiment. But state law makes it difficult for a municipality to change its current zoning along innovative lines.

First of all, Chapter 40A imposes a super-majority voting requirement on municipalities that wish to change existing zoning laws. A two-thirds vote of the city or town council, or a two-thirds vote of a town meeting, is required before any zoning by-law or ordinance—or any amendment to an existing zoning by-law or ordinance—can take effect. A proposed by-law or ordinance that fails to meet this voting requirement cannot be considered again for two-years unless it is recommended in the final report of the Planning Board.[15]

Chapter 40A also makes it difficult in other ways for a town or city in the Boston region to revamp its land use policies. In order to ensure that property owners are adequately notified about potential zoning changes, Chapter 40A has set a strict timeline that must be followed before any zoning change can go into effect.[16] This timeline provides property owners more than simply notice of local action. It also exempts them from the changes ultimately adopted by giving them a vested right to develop their land under the existing law. If property owners submit a definitive plan to the local planning board before the passage of new zoning regulations—even if they only submit a preliminary plan followed within seven months by a definitive plan—the plan is evaluated based upon the zoning laws in effect at the time of the submission and not the zoning regulations about to be passed.[17] All states recognize the vested interests of property owners that result from reliance on current zoning plans. But this Massachusetts procedure protects a vested right very early in the planning process.

If all that Chapter 40A did was to protect the vested rights of developers who already intended to build, this procedure would still have a major impact on a municipality's power to control land use. Chapter 40A, however, not only protects potential developers but creates potential developers. This occurs, for example, when a city or town declares a moratorium on apartment construction so that it can refine or develop a plan for the community. From the perspective of landowners, a notice of such a moratorium can be seen as a threat to their property interests. The moratorium not only prohibits apartment development during its existence but may be a precursor to significant zoning changes affecting that type of development. In order to protect themselves from possible detrimental effects to their property interest, landowners thus submit a preliminary proposal for the development of apartments in order to "freeze" their vested rights according to the current zoning plan. Before the moratorium is even voted on, in other words, the municipality is flooded with development applications for the type of development that the municipality wants to use the moratorium to investigate.

This kind of surge in applications occurred in the town of Framingham in the 1970s, resulting in a wave of apartment development. It took nearly twenty years for the market to absorb all the apartments that were hurriedly planned and developed because of the proposed moratorium.[18] To be sure, the protections of Chapter 40A properly seek to balance the power of the municipality to zone with the vested rights of property owners to develop according to their plans. Nevertheless, by allowing developers' rights to vest simply with the submission of a preliminary plan, current zoning law increases the very kind of development that the municipality wants to regulate. In the end, not only are municipal planning attempts frustrated but the interest of developers may also be undermined. They are given an incentive to engage in defensive development even if they had no plans to build the development beforehand.

AFFORDABLE HOUSING

The affordable housing sections of the Regional Planning Law—Chapter 40B of the General Laws[19] —were enacted to combat the exclusionary local zoning practices that have precluded the construction of affordable housing. Massachusetts was the first state to enact legislation that required municipalities to open themselves up to affordable housing development. Not only did Massachusetts recognize the need for legislative action in this area before any other state, but Chapter 40B was a purely legislative effort made without judicial compulsion. Politically, then, Chapter 40B was a major step towards recognizing the need to remove the barriers that generate class-based spatial segregation in Massachusetts.

The impact of Chapter 40B on the affordable housing market is notable. Since its inception, 18,000 affordable housing units have been built pursuant to Chapter 40B procedures. Over 60 percent of the municipalities that had no affordable housing units at the time Chapter 40B passed have since had affordable housing constructed. Indeed, affordable housing has been built in 85 percent of all cities and towns in Massachusetts, compared to only 50 percent before the act was passed.[20] Of course, the 18,000 units of affordable housing produced

in the thirty years after the passage of Chapter 40B make up a very small percentage of all suburban development. And there is also no indication that
Chapter 40B has led to any significant relocation of urban minorities into suburban communities.[21] Nevertheless, Chapter 40B is widely considered a prime
example of legislative innovation aimed at addressing inter-local inequalities.

Most municipal officials we interviewed applauded the goals of Chapter
40B. But almost all of them objected to its effect on local power. There was an
early judicial challenge to Chapter 40B on the ground that it invaded local home
rule authority. The Supreme Judicial Court rejected the challenge, concluding
that although "the zoning power is one of a city's or town's independent municipal powers included [in Article 89, Section 6's] broad grant of powers to adopt
ordinances or by-laws for the protection of the public health, safety, and general
welfare," Chapter 40B falls within the "legislature's supreme power in zoning .
. . ."[22] Despite the court's ruling, Chapter 40B's operation on a local level has
continued to be the target of criticism for its disregard of local concerns. The
general consensus was that the Act allocated too much power to developers
without granting localities the resources or authority to act on their own.

How Chapter 40B Works

Chapter 40B provides an alternative zoning approval process when qualified
developers propose the construction of affordable housing developments.
Responding to the tactics that some localities had employed to exclude low and
moderate income housing projects, Chapter 40B promotes the construction of
these projects by making two important modifications to the usual zoning
approval process. First, it replaces the previous procedural requirements that had
forced developers to get permission from a number of local authorities with a
single approval. Developers need only apply for a comprehensive permit from
the local Zoning Board of Appeals.[23] Secondly, if the Zoning Board of Appeals
denies the application or conditions its acceptance on "uneconomic" requirements, the developer can petition the Housing Appeals Committee, a state
agency, for a local zoning override. If the Housing Appeals Committee determines than an override is appropriate, it can order a "builder's remedy"—that
is, direct the locality to issue the necessary approvals that would allow the development to proceed.[24]

The Housing Appeals Committee's review of a potential development
attempts to strike a balance between a locality's need for affordable housing and
local objections to the project being built on the proposed site. One of the elements of this balance provides that if a municipality's stock of low and moderate income housing is less than 10 percent of its housing units, this fact
constitutes "compelling evidence that the regional need for housing does in fact
outweigh the objections to the proposal."[25] The impact of the Housing Appeals
Committee on local zoning decisions is evident in its rate of overturning them.

Since the enactment of Chapter 40B, only 18 local Zoning Board of Appeals decisions have been upheld by the Housing Appeals Committee, while 94 have been overruled. The majority of the other petitions were settled in a negotiation between the locality and the developer after the Housing Appeals Committee heard the appeal.[26] These negotiated settlements suggest a degree of cooperation between developers and localities. But the denial rate of the Housing Appeals Committee gives developers a considerable negotiating advantage in these settlement discussions.

How 40B Frustrates Local Efforts for Affordable Housing

To promote affordable housing in Massachusetts, it may well be necessary to give the Housing Appeals Committee final word over local zoning decisions. A number of officials indicated they had little incentive apart from the Chapter 40B mandate to permit affordable housing, particularly for families. As an official from Franklin explained, the costs associated with new residential development are so great that "we're trying to keep people out of town." There were, to be sure, contrary views. An official from Duxbury argued that "if we had the power and the state made a more generic goal, we would be able to address it." Even if some mandate akin to the one now in place is needed to encourage communities to make affordable housing development possible, however, Chapter 40B's current procedures can be understood to undermine local concerns in undesirable ways. Some of the concerns expressed by municipal officials related to the limited negotiating power that local governments have when private developers plan to construct developments that would qualify under Chapter 40B. Others related to the ways in which Chapter 40B impedes local efforts to make more affordable housing available.

Comments from an official from Somerville reflected the first set of concerns. She was critical of most localities for failing to develop affordable housing, but she was equally critical of the affordable housing provisions themselves for failing to take into account legitimate local concerns. She noted that dense Chapter 40B developments often require a significant amount of infrastructure—such as roads, utilities, and services. But because Chapter 40B rarely takes this need for infrastructure into account, private developers and the state essentially mandate the necessary infrastructure, whether or not the municipality has the resources to pay for it. A town official from Franklin complained about the town's lack of negotiating power in the Chapter 40B process. Even though Franklin had instituted a building moratorium to consider resource allocation for local services, the official reported, developers used Chapter 40B to develop 100 units on five acres in town. The developers were able to increase the density of the development well over what would normally have been acceptable. Yet Franklin lacked the power to negotiate for a lower density even though, according to the official, the development is located in an unfavorable location without adequate public transportation. Other municipal officials objected to the fact that, because the Housing Appeals Committee's review is limited to a specific site and a specific project, it need not consider whether there is a better alternate site or whether there is a better way to satisfy the desires of all the parties involved. As a result, the municipality has little power to influence the type of development being proposed so long as its housing is below the state statutory threshold. A town official from Middleton put his criticism bluntly: affordable housing "compromise[es] underlying zoning . . . [and] results in a flood on the school system and leave towns shaking in their boots."

A different set of concerns related to the charge that, as a number of town officials complained, aspects of Chapter 40B undermine local efforts to fulfill the general goal of producing inexpensive housing units for low and moderate income occupants. These concerns are particularly troubling. They suggest that towns and cities in the region are concerned about the effect of Chapter 40B on their home rule not because they object to its goals but because they are unduly limited in their power to achieve them. In fact, the comments that emphasized these limitations on local authority suggest that there are aspects of state policy that do less to promote affordable housing development throughout the state than to expand the discretion of private developers to build on their own terms.

This criticism arises in part from the fact that housing is not considered "affordable housing" in Massachusetts simply by ascertaining the affordability of the housing. Developers can qualify for the remedies provided in Chapter 40B only if the housing project is subsidized by federal or state grants.[27] Developers proposing inexpensive housing units without state or federal aid have to seek conventional local zoning approval. Existing inexpensive housing units that were not constructed with government subsidies also do not count toward satisfying the requirement that 10 percent of a municipality's housing units be affordable.[28]

Several officials complained that the selective way in which Chapter 40B promotes affordable housing development unfairly penalizes local communities. Federal and state grants for affordable housing are generally offered to projects of substantial size. For this reason, Chapter 40B fails to protect, let alone encourage, small efforts to produce affordable housing. Besides, state and federal funding is limited and not always available. In recent years, available funding has in fact become increasingly rare. Critics contend that the affordability and availability of the units should be the focus, not whether the federal or state government is sponsoring the project. Under current rules, local communities' actual contribution to the state's affordable housing needs go unrecognized. A Melrose official observed that it is a "travesty . . . that Section 8 housing isn't counted in the affordable housing percentage for [Chapter] 40B."

The number of affordable units in any given project that Chapter 40B requires is also an important issue for localities. Most affordable housing developments are proposed and built by private developers seeking to make a profit.

The majority of these developments have been high-density apartment complexes or condominiums with only the minimum amount of units set aside for low- to moderate-income occupants. There are several reasons for this. Government subsidies that help developers with the purchase price or construction cost of the project itself are limited. Land prices in most areas needing affordable housing often exceed the cost established to qualify as affordable housing, and developers therefore rely on a higher density to make a profit. The same economic constraints compel developers to ensure that the upper limits of the affordable housing index make up as many units as possible, and that market-rate units are maximized as well. Local officials are resentful of such practices. These practices affect a community's character and place a strain on local resources and services while providing only the minimum number of affordable units for the community. Yet because such developments qualify under Chapter 40B, the municipality has little room for maneuver when the developments are proposed.

Preserving affordable housing within a locality once it has been built is also a major concern. An official in the town of Burlington complained that the system allowed developers to override local housing decisions, retain the minimum amount of affordable housing for twenty years, and then convert them to market rate condominiums to be sold at a substantial profit. As a result, the municipally not only loses the social benefits of the affordable units but also loses units that count towards their 10 percent requirement. A Somerville official expressed a similar concern that several affordable units were expiring, but, she added, the city has been successful in negotiating with the developers to find ways to convince them to preserve the status quo. Concerns such as these arise because affordable housing units that count towards a municipality's 10 percent requirement usually receive assistance from the state, and the typical state requirement set forth in its financing agreements with developers is that the developer must preserve the specified amount of affordable housing units for a minimum of twenty years. To the extent that developers can price their development to conform to market rates once that time limit expires, municipalities can be forced to accept large developments yet be hard pressed to increase or maintain their affordable housing stock over time.[29]

Other aspects of Chapter 40B also play a role in making the preservation of affordable housing difficult for localities. An official from Medfield complained that the town had tried to do their own affordable housing project to get Chapter 40B credit without being subject to a large-scale private-developer-driven development. Upon going to the state to get the local housing initiative credited as a Chapter 40B project, "[the state] started setting rules and regulations; you have do it the state way." In particular, the state forced the municipality to tie the resale appreciation price to the real estate market in the town rather than to income levels in Boston area, as Medfield had wanted. "What happened, not only in Medfield but several towns," the official continued, "[is that] a house that we sold at lottery in 1992 for $90,000 is now reselling as an affordable unit for $202,000. It's difficult for people to qualify for mortgages, given the income levels and the asset levels that the state allows. They've in effect made affordable housing unaffordable."

One indication of the minimal local role in the production of affordable housing the state permits is that, before recent changes to Chapter 40B were made in 1990, affordable housing sponsored or built through local initiative or grants did not even qualify as Chapter 40B affordable housing. Thus Chapter 40B originally gave local authorities no incentive to initiate affordable housing projects on their own without state or federal grants. Ironically, then, Chapter 40B penalized communities that attempted to exclude affordable housing units from being built in their community but did little to encourage or reward efforts by them to sponsor the very types of developments that Chapter 40B was enacted to support. Administrative changes adopted in 1990 now allow housing projects developed through "local housing initiatives" to qualify for the 10 percent requirement. If a municipality donates funds or land to developers, or initiates and facilitates the development process, all units within that project qualify as affordable housing.[30] These changes have convinced some localities to take a more proactive role in developing affordable housing. An official from Lincoln noted that the town willingly located a developer and donated land to it for the purpose of constructing affordable housing. It did so without any state involvement.

There are, however, two limitations on Chapter 40B's encouragement for localities to take the initiative on affordable housing. First, Chapter 40B provides localities an incentive to act but no resources to enable them to do so. Officials from Peabody, Hull, and Gloucester expressed a desire to initiate more affordable housing development but said that they could proceed only if they received state financial assistance. Secondly, the 1990 change in Chapter 40B was administrative rather than statutory. It is not clear whether the Housing Appeals Committee will count all local initiatives as part of the 10 percent requirement. A town official from Burlington stated that the town recently made an agreement with a developer to swap town land with private land so that it could construct an affordable housing complex for seniors on the private land. The deal was to be accomplished without state or federal involvement, and the town planned to ensure that the complex continued to remain affordable. But the state informed the town that this project would not count towards its 10 percent requirement.

Other Ways State Law Limits Local Affordable Housing

While Chapter 40B generally focuses on limiting local land use control in order to promote the availability of affordable housing, some state statutes authorize localities to pursue affordable housing regulation on their own. Section 9 of Chapter 40A, for example, enables localities to "provide for special permits authorizing increases in the permissible density of population or intensity of use in a proposed development" on the condition that the developer "provide . . . housing for persons of low or moderate income." Some special acts, usually passed in response to home rule petitions, provide additional authority. But other provisions of state law—including the Home Rule Amendment itself—set forth significant obstacles to local efforts to ensure that housing is available for low and moderate income residents.

The state's cities have sought to use their home rule power to pass ordinances designed to preserve or increase their stock of affordable housing. These efforts include attempts to establish rent control, regulate condominium conversions, and require developer set-asides of affordable units in new construction. The Supreme Judicial Court has ruled, however, that these measures are not within a locality's home rule authority. As a result, virtually every significant local strategy for promoting affordable housing has to be based on carefully specified state enabling legislation rather than undertaken pursuant to broader independent home rule powers. Much of this enabling legislation is enacted as special legislation in response to home rule petitions from particular localities. Yet even when municipalities successfully obtain this legislative permission, the requirement that they seek permission erodes the strength of home rule authority while expanding the scope of state preemptive legislation. The scope of state legislation expands, and the category of local initiatives authorized by home rule authority contracts. The more this dynamic occurs, the more likely it becomes that the courts will strike down other kinds of local legislation on the ground that it lacks explicit state support.

Local efforts to ensure the existence of affordable housing provide many examples of this pattern. One year after the passage of the Home Rule Amendment, Brookline attempted to enact a rent control ordinance. The Supreme Judicial Court struck down the ordinance, holding that rent control was an enactment of "private or civil law governing civil relationships" prohibited by section 7 of the Home Rule Amendment.[31] Absent an explicit delegation of power by the state, the court said, municipalities cannot engage in regulation of the landlord-tenant relationship. After that decision, the legislature responded by passing a state-wide enabling act allowing for local regulation of rents and evictions.[32] When that act expired, some municipalities petitioned for, and were granted, special legislation to allow them to continue rent control. Municipalities, like Brookline, were thus eventually allowed to act in the manner that they had originally planned. But the result of this way of achieving their goal was to make clear that rent control was outside of local control, a point made not only by the court ruling but also by the subsequent passage of the enabling act.

Most municipalities initially based their condominium conversion laws on the state-enabling legislation that authorized rent control. This strategy ensured that they had a state statute on which they could rely for authority. But it also meant that local efforts would be scrutinized by examining the enabling legislation rather than the municipalities' home rule power. The City of Cambridge was one of the municipalities that defended its condominium regulations in this way. At first this strategy protected the city from legal challenges. The Supreme Judicial Court found that requiring a permit prior to the removal of any rent controlled unit from the market was essential to the operation of the rent control enabling legislation and is "therefore conferred by implication in the rent control state."[33] Although Cambridge defended the ordinance as authorized by its home rule power, the court never assessed that claim because it found authority under the rent control statute. The fact that this was the way the courts affirmed Cambridge's legislation had a detrimental effect on a subsequent legal challenge to an amendment to the same ordinance. In the later case, Cambridge again relied on its implied authority from the rent control act, this time not even mentioning its home rule authority. The Supreme Judicial Court struck down the amendment because it extended the proposed regulation beyond the limits allowed by the statute. The court didn't consider whether the amendment was permissible under home rule because such a claim was not even advanced as an argument.[34]

Rent control was abolished by a state-wide referendum in 1994.[35] Several municipalities thereafter petitioned for enabling statutes to allow them to enact local condominium control regulations like those previously based on rent control statutes. Again, the legislature was responsive in granting that power. But enabling statutes, along with the legacy of rent control, continue to limit the scope of municipal initiatives. In 1999, the Supreme Judicial Court struck down an amendment to expand Boston's condominium conversion laws to protect both current and prospective tenants. The court found that this extension of protections exceeded the scope of the state enabling statute, and it also found that it frustrated the repeal of the rent control act.[36] Boston's ability to regulate condominium conversion under its home rule authority was never evaluated. By then, this kind of legislation had been so integrally tied to rent control that the issue was treated as completely under the control of the state. Efforts by Newton and Fall River to regulate efforts by property owners to convert rental units to condominiums were also invalidated for lack of home rule authority under the state constitution.[37]

Local attempts to create affordable housing by conditioning building permits on mandatory set-asides of affordable units have followed a similar pattern of court rejection and legislative adoption. When the city of Newton sought to mandate that certain developers promise to sell 10 percent of their units at below-market rental rates in order to get a building permit, the Supreme Judicial Court held that it was beyond their power to do so because the state had preempted the field by adopting the Zoning Act.[38] The court also found that the local aldermen, acting as a zoning board, were "without power to make important policy decisions involved in committing a municipality to a program of housing for low income or elderly persons."[39] As a result, the state responded by making the "important policy decision" of allowing municipalities to condition special permits granting density bonuses on certain conditions including affordable housing set-asides.[40] Once again, the limited scope of the enabling statue restricted municipal initiatives that deviated from its provisions. Recent proposals for state enabling legislation that would expand the scope of local inclusionary zoning power beyond that conferred in Chapter 40A have not been adopted by the state legislature.

THE COMMUNITY PRESERVATION ACT

The Community Preservation Act[41] is state enabling legislation that allows localities that accept it through a local referendum to increase local property taxes for the purpose of promoting open space, historical preservation, or affordable housing. Municipalities participating in this program can also receive financial grants from the state to supplement the funds they receive from the increase in property taxes. The state allocates 80 percent of its grant allocation as matching funds to complement what the locality has raised; the remaining 20 percent is allocated according to a formula that takes into account factors such as equalized valuations per capita and population.[42]

Although the Community Preservation Act was designed to promote affordable housing and historic preservation along with open space, it is generally known and utilized primarily as a vehicle for promoting open space.[43] In our interviews, most of the municipal officials referred to it as an open space initiative and failed to mention its other goals. A number of them expressed gratitude that the state provided them with this option. An official from Pembroke stated that it was "great that communities have the flexibility of adopting the Community Preservation Act. People would be happy to put a portion of their taxed into an open space fund." A Peabody official stressed the importance of basing the Act on a local option rather than a mandate. "Many communities," he said, "may not be able to afford this or may have already set aside sufficient resources." On the other hand, one official we interviewed noted that the Act in some ways reflects the lack of independent home rule authority that the state grants its cities and towns. A town administrator from Middleton saw the Community Preservation Act as an "example of the state trying to deal with home rule issues." He explained: if "home rule authority . . . really existed, [then] cities and towns wouldn't have to go through the charade of asking for a Community Preservation Act and then subsequently not adopt[ing] it. In my view, it's a failure."

The fact that the Community Preservation Act is a state law, rather than a local one, is important. It means that those aspects that are problematic from the perspective of local officials are beyond local power to change. Against this background, the fact that the majority of comments regarding the operations of the Community Preservation Act were critical once again reflects the way that state laws both confer land use power and limit it in important ways. Some officials articulated their dissatisfaction with the formula the Act uses to distribute the state grants. Officials from Somerville and Weston expressed concern that the formula led to an unfair redistribution of funds between rich and poor municipalities. The funds distributed by the state come from a surcharge applied to registry of deed filings. The surcharge does not vary from locality to locality, and there is no indication that registry filings favor rich municipalities over poor ones. But the disbursement formula allocates 80 percent of those surcharges back to participating municipalities as a matching fund. As a result, even though a wealthy locality may not collect a significant amount for registry filings, it will receive a larger state distribution because the money is allocated in proportion to property tax rates. Perhaps the formula was designed to allocate more money to municipalities where open space and affordable housing are more expensive due to inflated property prices. Nevertheless, as an official from Weston observed, its effect is to take from poor communities and give to rich ones.

Others we interviewed expressed frustration with the competing goals facing municipalities when they consider protecting open space. One such conflict is between the need for open space and the need for revenue. According to a Wilmington official, revenue restrictions like Proposition 2½ "makes the town more reluctant to preserve open space in a way that would take it off their tax rolls." An official from Melrose articulated this tension by explaining the city's current struggle with this issue: "A condominium complex was recently proposed . . . [it] would bring . . . in $1.2 million in taxes each year. That's a huge amount for us. But there is a serious internal debate in Melrose about the trade-offs between revenue and controlling sprawl."

As noted above, the passage of the Community Preservation Act offers municipalities a means to raise resources for the support of affordable housing initiatives as well as to preserve open space. Some officials expressed concerns about what they perceive as a conflict between these two goals. A locality that purchases and sets aside open space will, by doing so, eliminate from development land that might have been available for affordable housing. In fact, an official from Somerville noted, the Act is often used for the purpose of buying a specific parcel of land to avoid a potential affordable housing development. She noted that a referendum will sometimes be introduced and approved right after a controversial development has been proposed. A town administrator from Ashland illustrated this conflict when he said that it was often cheaper to "buy land and make it open space than to allow developers to build housing on it, have kids move into the housing and make the town expand its school system." Although he was not specifically referring to the Community Preservation Act or to affordable housing, he nevertheless articulates the concerns of municipal administrators faced with these options. The current legal structure promotes this kind of defensive use of the Community Preservation Act. Because municipalities lack control over the development of their community in other ways, they often feel compelled to rely on the Community Preservation Act to resist development. This defensive use of the Act undermines, rather than fosters, local attempts to prepare a well thought out master plan that incorporates state requirements along with local concerns. As a result, plans for open space may be adopted without a serious consideration of the need for it or of its impact on other interests of the community.

Another tension within the structure of the Community Preservation Act is between the referendum procedure the Act mandates[44] and its goal of helping localities develop affordable housing. The Act offers municipal governments the ability to develop and construct affordable housing units with their own resources and on their own terms. It thus offers another way to achieve Chapter 40B's objective of eroding exclusionary zoning practices. But many of these exclusionary practices have considerable local support. If so, it is counterproductive to give municipalities the resources to meet the affordable housing requirement only if it is passed in a referendum. Not surprisingly, it is hard for a municipal government to convince constituents to accept a tax increase to support projects that they do not want constructed in the first place. The town of Carlisle, governing through open town meetings, attempted to address its affordable housing issue on a number of occasions, but every time the issue came before the town meeting it was voted down. The same kind of local opposition occurred in Acton when the town wanted to convert an old vacant schoolhouse into affordable housing units. Parents rallied against the proposal because they did not want affordable housing close to the new schoolhouse.

The effect on efforts to build affordable housing is only one of the reasons why it matters that the Community Preservation Act requires referendum approval before a municipality can take advantage of its provisions. This structure prevents the municipal government itself from taking advantage of the Act. Once again, as with many other issues mentioned above (such as Proposition 2½ overrides), a state law disempowers elected local officials on an important policy issue by shifting the locus of decision making to the electorate. This allocation of power has significant consequences: as of May 2003, only 61 out of the 109 communities that have taken final action on the legislation enacted the Community Preservation Act.[45] Hull is one of the communities that failed to pass the act; one official thought this was because "citizens are not concerned with this issue."

LAND USE REGULATIONS AND LOCAL GOVERNMENT

The Community Preservation Act's allocation of power to the local electorate, rather than to elected municipal officials, may seem an appropriate way to define local control. But it would be a mistake to think that this structure gives the local population the final say on land use matters. The state, after all, retains the power to make land use decisions. When the local electorate's wishes conflict with state policy, the state can—and does—override local decision making. The effect of the referendum structure is not to empower local constituents against state decisions. Its effect is to undermine the role of municipal officials. Yet even though a significant number of municipal land use decisions are made by the state or by local constituents, the municipal government is generally treated as responsible for local land policy. Whenever that policy runs contrary to the (often conflicting) interests of the state and the electorate, municipal officials take the blame.

This dynamic is evident for each of the municipal land use issues discussed above. The Zoning Act seems to grant municipalities broad latitude to control land use. But the state not only exempts itself from local zoning rules but disperses the zoning power to a wide range of different groups. Unlike the standard procedure used when other by-laws or ordinances are enacted, zoning laws can be considered only after the public has been notified and heard and only after the local zoning board issues a recommendation. Moreover, decisions to change zoning laws may be blocked by a minority of locally elected officials or even by the claims of private property owners asserting the generous vested rights state law grants them. This dispersal of authority makes it possible for individual constituents and the state to frustrate a proposed zoning law even before it has been voted on. It also undermines municipal officials' attempts to accomplish their planning goals while, at the same time, continuing to make them responsible for the lack of an adequate land use policy in the eyes of their electorate.

Chapter 40B imposes similar limitations on municipal government's ability to act. Enacted with the purpose of overcoming local exclusionary zoning techniques, Chapter 40B diverts power away from municipal governments but holds them accountable for the lack of results. Affordable housing projects are initiated by the private sector, and the requirements for these projects rely on obtaining state or federal grants. The local Zoning Board of Appeals has an opportunity to review the affordable housing application, but it is required to hold public hearings to gather the views of local constituents. Since there is often little local support for affordable housing in the communities that need it, the decisions of the zoning board often attempts to strike a compromise between the mandates of the state and the wishes of the constituents. Yet if the private developer has an issue with this compromise, it can appeal to the Housing Appeals Committee for review. In this review, the state agency can override any compromise. In the end, the state may well be frustrated with the locality because it sees it as trying to torpedo the affordable housing project. The private developer may well be frustrated with the zoning board for the same reason. And the constituents may well be frustrated because they feel their interests are being neglected. Even though the tension in this scenario can be described as being between the constituents of a locality, the developer, and the state government, it is likely that all three of them will point to the municipal government as the root of their frustrations. This phenomenon reinforces the idea that more checks on municipal power are needed.

Finally, as we have seen, municipal governments have little power to preserve affordable housing once it has been built. Rent control has been abolished, and condominium conversion regulation requires the express permission of the state. Because most low and moderate income occupants rent rather than buy, localities thus do not have power to assist the people who most need the affordable housing. Even state subsidies for affordable housing require only that the units stay affordable for 20 years. When that time limit has elapsed, affordable housing can be, and often is, sold at market price. Municipalities, then, are penalized for not meeting the 10 percent requirement even though they are given little power to preserve their affordable housing stock once it has been built.

Efforts have been made to untie the hands of municipal governments on affordable housing issues. But these efforts have also been subjected to state-imposed restrictions. Although the Housing Appeals Committee now allows affordable housing developed with local assistance to qualify for the 10 percent requirement, municipalities have been given no resources to build the housing. The Community Preservation Act is an attempt to overcome this lack of resources by allowing municipalities to collect additional property tax that can be used to subsidize affordable housing developments. But a city or town can use the powers that the Act authorizes only if their constituents approve a tax increase through a local referendum. Because the root of municipal opposition to affordable housing often originates in the constituents themselves, it has been difficult for the municipalities that need affordable housing to convince their constituents to accept a tax increase to help build it. Once again, decision making power over the preservation and construction of affordable housing is allocated to the state or the local electorate, with the municipal government relegated to the status of a disempowered mediator between these two interests.

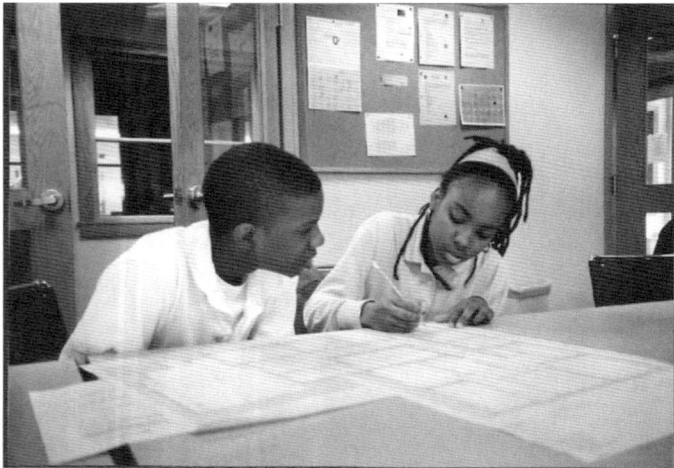

4. Home Rule in Action: Education

"The town has no control really over the schools. The school committee sets broad guidelines and controls operation. The town meeting does approve the school committee's budget, but they have no control over where the money goes, how many teachers go where, and what programs are funded and how much."

—Public official from Arlington

Of all the services that municipal governments offer, education is the one that is most commonly seen as a local issue. These days, however, the growing demand for better education, combined with the increasing popularity of alternatives to public schools, have altered the connection between education and local communities. These developments have not eliminated the influence local officials have over the public schools. But they have made even clearer what had already been the case: that local officials do not have anything like autonomous control over the schools within their borders.

No one would dispute the intrinsic value of education. But municipalities care about education for reasons other than the importance they rightly place on instructing their young people. They recognize that the quality of education is inextricably connected to the perceived "value" of their municipality. Most families looking for homes factor a city or town's perceived educational quality into the purchase price of the house they buy. Homes are often chosen as much for the value of the community and its environment as for the value of the house itself. As a result, property values, from which property taxes are derived, imply and encompass the cost of the education provided within the municipality. A demonstration of this inter-relationship can be seen in the impact that objective measures of educational quality have on municipal growth, development, and revenue. After the Massachusetts Comprehensive Assessment System (MCAS)[1] results of 2002 were announced, realtors in Walpole were eager to begin using their town's recent climb to give them an edge in pitching their property. Similarly, town officials in Rockport, whose rank climbed from 101st to 51st in the state, were hopeful that "property values will similarly climb."[2]

Just as education affects development and property values, development and property values affect education. Education is funded primarily on a local level,[3] and educational quality is thus significantly tied to property tax receipts. Even though the state has sought to minimize school inequality by distributing state aid to equalize educational funding, older municipalities with a small local tax base (such as Salem and Lynn) still spend less than the regional average.[4] Studies indicate that rapidly developing bedroom communities also spend below the regional average per student (Boxborough and Northborough are examples).[5] A town official from Wilmington told us how the "growth of the town during the 1990s put a lot of pressure on the schools," a fact that has "presented a financial problem." On a related point, officials from Middleton and Somerville noted that the fear that uncontrolled growth would put pressure on local schools contributed to the criticism of Chapter 40B's affordable housing requirement.

Given this important inter-relationship between education and municipal vitality, it is significant that—with the important exception of Boston itself—cities and towns do not control their own schools. Instead, under state law, schools are under the control of elected school committees—committees that are sometimes elected by the residents of a single municipality and sometimes operated on a regional basis. This fracturing of the local government structure between municipalities and school committees raises the question of what "home rule" on education issues might mean in Massachusetts. This question will be explored in the first section below. We then turn to the extent of local control on educational issues even by school committees. Because the quality of education has become an ever more important issue for the Commonwealth of Massachusetts, the role of the state in establishing educational policy has become increasingly significant. The result, epitomized by the Educational Reform Act of 1993, has been to subject local school committees and local schools to more rigid state requirements. Finally, we analyze another important development affecting the extent of local power on education issues—the rise of charter schools. At one level, charter schools can be seen as competitors to the local public schools: they are innovative alternatives funded by the locality in which the student lives. On another level, charter schools are part of the public education system itself. The state requires, for example, that municipalities provide transportation for school children attending charter schools. Here, again, the state plays a dramatic role in determining educational policy that significantly affects the region's localities.

SCHOOLS AND THE MUNICIPALITY

The relationship between education and the municipality is circular and symbiotic: education affects how the municipality develops and is itself affected by the growth that it influences. Yet in Massachusetts, school committees rather than municipalities are responsible for the management of local public schools. Unless otherwise provided for by law, school committees consist of three or more members elected at large. They are independent governing bodies within a municipality (or, in the case of a regional school district, several municipalities).[6] Except in the City of Boston, they are not under the control of city government. (In some cities, either because they follow a standard plan or because—as in Malden—

they have obtained special legislation, the mayor has a permanent seat on the committee.) School committees have the power, within the bounds established by state statutes or the Department of Education, to operate the public schools. They regulate student attendance, set the curriculum, hire and fire teachers and other employees, and determine when schools should be closed. Cities and towns do not have the power to do any of these things.

The political isolation of school committees from municipalities is intentional. As the Massachusetts Supreme Judicial Court explained: "The policy of the commonwealth from early times has been to establish a board elected directly by the people separate from other governing boards . . . and to place the control of the public schools within the jurisdiction of that body unhampered as to the details of administration and not subject to review by any other board or tribunal . . . ."[7] Of course, despite the breadth of this language, school committees are very much under the supervision of the state Department of Education. The body that seems to be primarily separated from the school committees, then, is the municipality.

The fractured relationship between school committees and the municipalities they serve raises questions about the definition of "local" control of schools. In earlier parts of this report, we noted the split in the way the "local" will is determined between decisions made by the municipal government and by referendum. Here, we note another split: between municipal government and other kinds of local government institutions. Education is by no means the only issue under the control of a state-created institution separate from the elected municipal government. (Transportation is an example, among many others, of an issue allocated to public authorities rather than to municipal governments.) Education is unusual, however, because school committees, unlike other state-created institutions, are popularly elected. Still, the fact that they are legally splintered from municipal governments complicates the question whether they properly embody the notion of local control of education. School committees tend to work more closely with the state Department of Education than with municipal officials or the public at large. And they have more formal contacts with, and are subject to more regulations by, the state than is the city or town government. If the school committee and municipal officials disagree about educational policy—and if both views diverge from public opinion within the municipality as a whole— which of the three positions represents the "local" point of view?

The division between municipal governments and school committees has additional significant consequences for the relevance of the concept of home rule to education issues. School committees are responsible for school management, but they are not given home rule power by the Home Rule Amendment. Only cities and towns are given home rule power by the Home Rule Amendment. Yet, except in Boston, cities and towns do not run the schools. Thus, to put the matter simply: except in Boston, there is no "home rule" in Massachusetts as far as education is concerned.[8]

There are, however, two important legally structured relationships between school committees and municipalities: the approval of the annual budget and of school construction projects. School committees are required to submit a budget proposal to the municipality, and the city council or the town meeting can approve or modify the total amount of funds requested in the budget. But the law makes clear that the municipal legislature cannot fine-tune the budget; it can do no more than make nonbinding recommendations:

> In acting on appropriations for educational costs, the city or town appropriating body shall vote on the total amount of the appropriations requested and shall not allocate appropriations among accounts or place any restrictions on such appropriations. . . . The city or town may make nonbinding monetary recommendations to increase or decrease certain items allocating such appropriations. The vote of the legislative body of a city or town shall establish the total appropriation for the support of the public schools, but may not limit the authority of the school committee to determine expenditures within the total appropriation.[9]

School construction is also under the general purview of the municipal administration because it deals with land use issues and requires budgetary allocations outside of the general operating expenses of the schools.

Given that the primary intersection between municipal administrators and school committees concerns budget approvals, it is no surprise that financial support was the focus of almost all the education-related comments of the municipal officials we interviewed. Many municipal administrators were critical of policymakers for equating educational funding and educational quality. But others talked about the success of their schools in terms of the percentage of the municipal budget that has been allocated to them (Acton, Carlisle, Concord, Hamilton). This focus on educational funding as the benchmark for educational quality is illustrative of the deep split between the administration of local schools and other aspects of municipal governance.

Despite the importance of education to the welfare of the municipality, educational policies, programs, and curricula were rarely mentioned in our interviews. Some officials (from Marblehead and Somerville, for example) simply noted that they were not in a position to comment on education issues because education was under the purview of the school committees. Others directly commented on their lack of control or formal relationship with the local school committee. They noted that appointments of the leading educational officials in the district, from principal to superintendent, are essentially beyond the authority of the municipality. In the words of an official from Arlington:

The town has no control really over the schools. The school committee sets broad guidelines and controls operations. The town meeting does approve the school committee's budget, but they have no control over where the money goes, how many teachers go where, and what programs are funded and how much. Town meeting can approve or reduce the budget without altering anything within the budget. The town can control which schools get renovated first or what schools are built, but the operations are under the control of the school committee.

An official from Hull echoed this vision, stating that the primary "interaction is between the elected school board and the [state] Department of Education. Local power is limited.'

The splintering of authority between the school committee and the municipality does more than limit the power of cities or towns to play an active role in influencing educational quality. It also creates confusion about who is responsible for improving the quality of local services unrelated to education. A large portion of a city's or town's expenditures is often used to pay for education to satisfy a school committee's budget request. That sizeable appropriation leaves the city or town with comparatively little revenue to spend on other local services. Local residents may nonetheless feel that they have spent a considerable amount of money in taxes with little to show for it. They then blame the city or town officials both for the failings they perceive in the local school system (which the city or town does not control) and for the inadequacy of other local services (which cities or towns may underfund in order to meet the budget request of the school committee). This dynamic led a respondent from Acton to argue that the state should establish two separate taxing systems, one administered by the town for non-education-related services and one administered by the school committees to pay for their budgets. On this view, towns and cities would be better off if they did not have to raise revenues to pay for education given the minimal influence on educational policy state law gives them. Such a system would ensure "that we don't get held accountable for other stuff when all of the money goes to schools."

As noted above, Boston is in some respects an exception to the general structure just described.[10] In 1991, after the citizens of Boston had approved a nonbinding referendum supporting the change, the state legislature approved Boston's home rule petition replacing its elected school committee with a seven-person committee appointed by the mayor. The City of Boston thus has an unusual amount of control over its schools. But that control is limited even by the terms of the legislation that authorized the creation of the appointed committee. The state legislation specified (among other things) that the new school committee have seven members, that the members have staggered terms of office, and that there be a 13-member nominating panel (organized in detail by the legislation) empowered to present a list of candidates from which the mayor selects committee members. This structure can only be modified by another state legislative enactment. Given this state-defined structure, it would be an over-statement to suggest that, even in Boston, the city has the kind of control over education that it can exercise over other issues.

SCHOOLS AND THE STATE

Education in Massachusetts is a duty imposed upon the state government by the state constitution.[11] Although much of that duty has been delegated to school committees, the state—namely, the state Department of Education and the state Board of Education—retains significant control over the way in which school committees provide education to their constituents. In an earlier section of this report, we referred to the fact that the Education Reform Act established a min-imum level of funding for every school district in the state.[12] In this section, we concentrate on another important ingredient in the Education Reform Act: the Act contains a host of mandates designed to improve school quality and account-ability throughout the state.

Under the Act, the Department and Board of Education are required to establish curriculum frameworks in the core subjects of mathematics, science and technology, history and social sciences, English, foreign languages, and the arts.[13] They are authorized to provide standards for subjects ranging from nutrition to the Federalist Papers and from computer skills to AIDS. (The legislature itself has mandated education on subjects ranging from the bill of rights to physical edu-cation.)[14] They set educator certification standards, provide for the length of the school day and school year, and have the power to declare a school district "under-performing" and, if so, intervene in its operation.[15] And, most famously, they have established the Massachusetts Comprehensive Assessment System (MCAS). These are simply examples of the multitude of state-wide requirements for teachers and students imposed by the state. Even though school committees have significant control over the day-to-day operations of their schools, the Education Reform Act has thus moved education a significant way towards state control of education. (In 2002, the No Child Left Behind Act[16] increased federal intervention into school policy as well.)

Many of the most controversial state-generated educational mandates do not arise directly out of legislative decisions. They derive instead from requirements imposed on school committees through administrative decisions by the Department of Education. Many of these decisions take advantage of municipal dependence on state aid. One of the most controversial educational standards is the implementation of the MCAS as the state-wide graduation requirement for all students wishing to receive a high school degree. Although a testing and assessment regime like the MCAS was adopted by the legislature as a part of the

Educational Reform Act, the Act simply identified the test as a tool to compare municipal education quality, help formulate better educational programs, and "inform teachers, parents, administrators and the students themselves, as to individual academic performance."[17] The Department of Education, however, has formally requested that local school districts adopt the MCAS as an official and uniform graduation requirement—a request that comes in a tone more like that of a mandate than a choice. Financial dependence renders localities vulnerable to these kinds of requests. As the Boston Globe put it: "The state Department of Education has issued a stern warning: Comply or you could face punitive action—a visit from the attorney general or the loss of state and federal funds."[18] There are also indications that state aid has created a sense of moral or psychological indebtedness to the state. A Manchester official expressed this idea by stating: "I have tremendous difficulty with school systems that say 'we are part of the state system' and accept state funding, and then refuse to do what the [state] regulations require."[19] Even though the merits of the MCAS are still widely debated, it is clear that the debate is not a local debate.[20]

Most of the municipal officials we interviewed were critical of the state's involvement in education. Much of this criticism was directed at state educational mandates, especially those that required municipal spending but did not guarantee state reimbursements. These officials stressed that other programs would have to be sacrificed to comply with the state requirements. A town administrator from Medfield, after noting the town's reliance on state educational funding, disapproved of the multitude of reports the town must file documenting everything on which they spend their money. The town is not even allowed to establish its tax rate, he said, until the Department of Education certifies that enough money was being spent on education. A spokesman for Peabody, expressing concerns about the difficulties of budgeting the town's funds in accordance with state requirements, argued that the municipalities should be able to determine the standards and shape of their schools. This sentiment mirrored that of an official from Pembroke when he asked: "Shouldn't Pembroke make the decisions of how much money they want to spend on their school system?"

In addition to comments on how state restrictions affect municipal budgets, there were also remarks regarding the state's control of education itself. An administrator from Salem, although receptive to the idea that the state should establish general guidelines and parameters in education, said that actual decision making regarding the implementation of those guidelines "must be a bottom-up arrangement." An official from Gloucester stated that "the state definitely intrudes more than they should . . . it's not good to have every community in lock-step . . . [but that] is where Massachusetts seems to be going." Rigidity was also an issue for Medfield: "[The state has] one approach for everyone; what works in Chelsea probably won't work in Medfield, but they don't give us any flexibility."

An official from Cohasset said simply that he was of the opinion that there is "not many local powers to deal with education."

Many municipal officials recognized that the state was a significant partner in providing funds for education and school-related development. In order to equalize the disparities between municipal fiscal capacity, they pointed out, the state provides aid under a need-based formula that attempts to help all schools meet the required spending minimum. There is also significant state support for building new schools and renovating existing schools.[21] Like other situations in which state aid is involved, municipal reaction to this aid was mixed. Some municipal officials, like one from Lynn, were grateful to the state for providing much needed resources: "With this funding, Lynn has had the power and resources to make significant improvements in education." A city official from Medford also praised the "generousness" of the state in providing more resources to their city. Others, although happy to get state aid and resources, recognized the limitations imposed by state grants. A spokesman for Peabody commented on potential problems arising since state aid is "being cut and the time before cities are reimbursed is getting longer."

It is worth re-emphasizing that, although the state regulates a school's curriculum, spending, and teacher qualification requirements, important aspects of school operations are still independently regulated by school committees. In some areas, school committees are given more latitude than the municipality itself. Cambridge, for example, recently became one of the few municipalities in the nation to begin desegregating their schools primarily on the basis of economic status rather than race.[22]

LOCAL PUBLIC SCHOOLS AND ALTERNATIVES

This report has already noted that, in addition to the consolidation of educational policy in the hands of the state, there is a splintering of local educational responsibility between municipalities (the budget) and school committees (managing the schools). The splintering of local public education, however, is not limited to the relationship between the municipality and the school committee. It is also now in evidence in the relationship between local public schools and charter schools. Here, too, state law sharply limits the control that municipalities have over what is perhaps the most important service provided within their borders.

Charter schools are not the only mechanism Massachusetts has adopted to expand the local educational options available to students and parents. The state has also established a school choice program designed to allow students to enroll in out-of-district schools as long as the receiving school committee has places available and is willing to receive them.[23] But charter schools are an even more pervasive educational alternative. In 2001, there were 43 charter schools in Massachusetts.[24] These charter schools have expanded the educational options beyond the traditional public school in ways that have produced significant benefits. At the same time, they are one more indication that the traditional concept of a locally controlled educational regime is being transformed.

Massachusetts state law authorizes two different types of charter schools.[25] A "commonwealth charter school" is a public school, proposed and sponsored by teachers, parents, or a non-profit business or corporate entity, that operates under a charter issued by the state Board of Education. Commonwealth charter schools are governed by an independent board of trustees and operate "independently of any school committee."[26] A "Horace Mann charter school" is a public school proposed by a local school committee; it can even be a subdivision of an existing public school. The charter of a Horace Mann charter school is also granted by the state Board of Education and it too is operated by a board of trustees "independent of the school committee" that sponsors it.[27] Neither the municipal government nor the school committee, then, has formal influence over either kind of charter school.

Even though the state—rather than the city or town where the charter school is located—determines whether a charter school may open, charter schools have a significant impact on the municipal budget. State law ensures that every student that charter schools admit reduces the local educational aid received by the municipality. This draining of local aid results from a complex state-established formula transferring a portion of that aid from the school committee to the charter school where that student is enrolled. Local school committees have been critical of the current formula on the grounds that it neglects the fact that the cost of maintaining a school cannot be reduced to per-pupil spending—losing one student, and the funds associated with that student, does not save the public school the amount being transferred. Moreover, since high school students are more expensive to educate than K–8 students, and since most charter schools have concentrated on K–8 education, the formula gives charter schools more than a traditional public K–8 school would be allocated for the same students.[28]

Despite the fact that charter schools are administratively outside the control of both municipal governments and local school committees, they are public schools. Their employees and administrators are agents of the state; they are subject to most of the same rules applicable to other public schools; they cannot discriminate in admissions on the grounds of traditional categories like race or sex or on the grounds of academic achievement; they must give admissions preference to students from the city or town in which they are located; they are funded by the city or town budget. Students attending charter schools are also entitled to public transportation administered and financed by municipal governments.[29]

Notwithstanding this classification of charter schools as public schools, a municipality's interaction with them is more restricted than its interaction with the traditional local public schools. The boards of trustees for charter schools are not elected at large. As a result, they are not accountable to the citizenry of the municipality as a whole. Moreover, charter schools are even more under state control than are school committees. Although they set their own education policies (within the bounds established by the state), their charters are granted by the state and their budget allocated according to state formulas. Moreover, their charters last only for five years and are subject to being revoked:

> The board [of education] may revoke a school's charter if the school has not fulfilled any conditions imposed by the board in connection with the grant of the charter or the school has violated any provision of its charter. The board may place the charter school on a probationary status to allow the implementation of a remedial plan after which, if said plan is unsuccessful, the charter may be summarily revoked.[30]

Both the independence of charter schools from the municipality and their connection to the state thus increases the fragmentation that characterizes the formulation of educational policy for the public schools in the Boston region.

These observations are not meant to disparage the benefits that charter schools offer by providing children with alternative educational opportunities. Nor are they designed to undermine the value charter schools provide traditional public schools when, as required by state law, they share their experimental models with the public schools at large. The point being made here is more limited. Like the separation of school committees from municipal governments and like the influence of the state on educational policy, charter schools make problematic the relevance of the concept of "home rule" in the context of education.

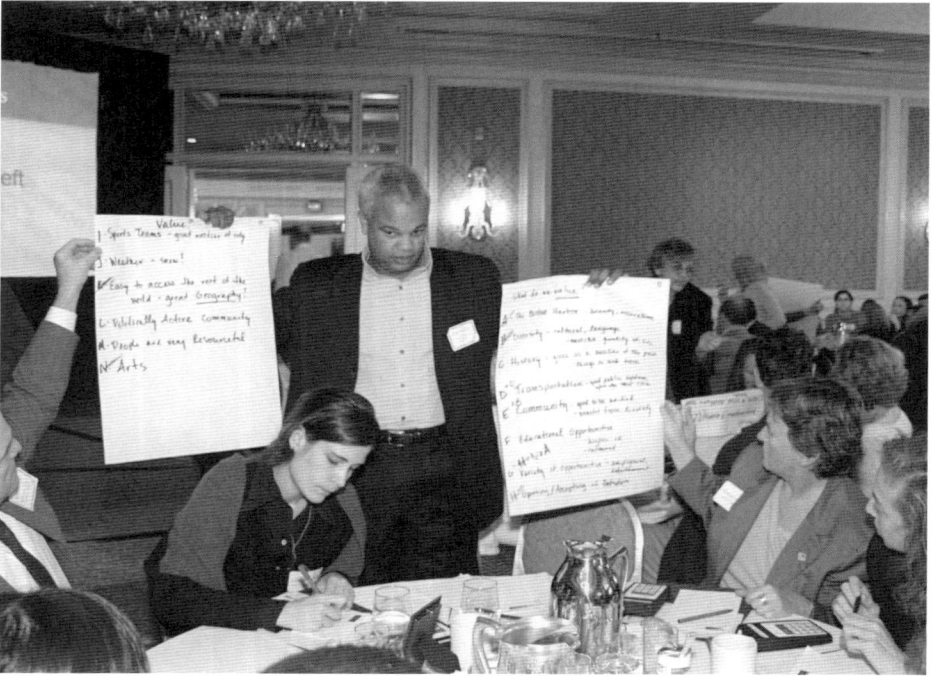

5. Thinking as a Region

"Municipalities in the region suffer from the belief that those people over there, they're four miles away, [and] they're different than us. . . . We've failed in local government to be willing to take on the idea of more efficiency and effectiveness by going outside our physical boundaries."

—Public official from Franklin

We have seen that Massachusetts places significant limits on the home rule of the 101 cities and towns in the Boston region. These limits range from the substantial exceptions to their general home rule authority set forth in the state constitution, to the pervasive shadow of state preemption, to state statutes that restrict municipal authority over budgeting, land use, and education. These limits do not go unnoticed by those charged with exercising local power. Comments from local officials quoted throughout this report testify to their understanding that, in many respects, home rule does not exist in Massachusetts in any meaningful sense.

Yet, for all their complaints about the illusory nature of home rule, the region's local officials do not regard it as unimportant. There is no better indication of this than the answers they gave to questions about the benefits of regionalism. Even though relatively few officials suggested that home rule authority was strong in Massachusetts, a large number referred to its importance in response to questions about regionalism. Some who spent much of their interview emphasizing the state's dominant role—and the relatively trivial amount of power that it had left to cities and towns—made an abrupt about face when it came to regionalism. Suddenly, the power of the city or town to control its future—a power that they had earlier suggested had effectively been taken from them—was at risk of being lost.

The prevalence of this mindset might be thought to support the conventional view that the attachment to home rule makes progress in addressing regional concerns unlikely in Massachusetts. This conclusion seems to us too simple. As many of those interviewed noted, the decisions made by the region's cities and towns affect their neighbors even on issues traditionally considered local in scope. This inter-local effect is obvious when one considers the three issues just discussed: revenue, land use, and education. Attempts to attract businesses and residents in an effort to increase property values produce a parallel downturn in the municipalities left behind. Encouraging commercial development causes traffic problems across the border, and efforts to prevent the development of multi-family housing force potential residents to move to municipalities that accept it or already have it. Comparisons about educational quality help some municipalities at the expense of others, while students, however educated, move from one part of the region to another. And it's not just the municipalities that are inter-connected. Transportation systems, business transactions, television networks, and environmental impacts also do not stop at municipal boundaries, and residents who live and vote in one municipality shop, work, and party in others.

Because of these interconnections, many officials agreed that a municipality's ability to address its problems depends on more than its ability to regulate the affairs that occur within its own borders. A locality's ability to react to its residents' needs depends in important respects on its ability to coordinate, communicate, and cooperate with other cities and towns within the region. Any analysis of home rule in the Boston region would be incomplete, therefore, without an account of the ability of cities and towns within it to think and act regionally.

In the remaining sections of this report, we address the complex relationship between home rule and regionalism revealed by our examination of the state's legal structure and our interviews with local officials. We begin by describing the understanding of the relationship between home rule and regionalism that emerged from the interviews. We then consider the role that state law plays both in enabling and frustrating the ability of cities and towns in the region to work with each other. We conclude by examining some ways in which the state might promote regionalism while, at the same time, enhancing home rule.

ATTITUDES ABOUT REGIONALISM AND HOME RULE

One reason so many officials perceive regionalism as a threat to home rule relates to a key finding that emerged from our interviews: there is little sense that the boundaries of the Boston region define a community of shared interest. The region we examined is very large. Its borders contain upwards of 3 million people (more than half the state's population) and span more than 1,400 square miles. Within that space are "coastal communities, older industrial centers, rural towns, and modern cities."[1] Most of the municipal officials to whom we spoke saw little in common with cities or towns in the region that were far from them, different in size, or different in community character. They often described cooperative efforts from a perspective that assumed a competitive division between the city and the suburbs, or inner-ring suburbs and outer-ring suburbs, or the North Shore and Metro West, or their own town's population and that of their neighbors.

The reluctance to join with other towns to form regional school districts provides an example of this phenomenon. State law authorizes inter-local agreements establishing regional school districts,[2] and their creation would save many localities money. Yet the attachment to local control over public schools—along with the general atmosphere of inter-municipal competition—makes efforts to form regional school districts difficult. A Medway official said that in Massachusetts "everyone seems to want their own schools and there's a lot of competition." In some municipalities, constituents oppose regional school systems because it would result in a diverse student body. A Medfield official stated that the town "looked at regional schools at one point," but the possibility was promptly defeated by "snobby attitudes from communities including this one: 'We don't want our kids going to school with kids from Sherborn and Millis.'" According to an official from Franklin, these attitudes about schooling reflect a deeper sensibility. Municipalities in the region, he explained, suffer from the belief "that those people over there, they're four miles away, [and] they're different than us . . . . We've failed in local government to be willing to take on the idea of more efficiency and effectiveness by going outside our physical boundaries."

When regional thinking does occur, the municipal officials we interviewed tended to identify with smaller sub-regions within the region rather than the region as a whole. To the extent they saw benefits to regionalism, they agreed with an administrator from Bedford who described regional cooperation as occurring primarily "with the immediately surrounding towns." The general sentiment was that this compact definition of the region better accounted for the shared problems, desires, and goals of the individual municipalities involved. In one telling comment, an official of a relatively small North Shore town expressed enthusiasm for establishing greater connections with the large city in the region, but the city that this official had in mind was Gloucester, not Boston.

In contrast to their affinity for these small clusters of communities, respondents saw the boundaries defined by regional planning agencies and county-based administration as arbitrary and over-inclusive. A Duxbury official explained: "The cooperation among municipalities has always been perverted, in my opinion, because there were these arbitrary boundaries . . . called counties or called regional planning agencies that had nothing to do with the communities themselves. We wanted [to cooperate] by contiguous boundaries, where the towns have some of the same needs." A respondent from Medway agreed that county lines and broad regional boundaries grouped together communities that had little in common. He supported localities taking regional concerns into account but not "on a county basis—Medway is a part of Norfolk County, but we have little in common with towns like Quincy and Braintree. I would want it on a smaller and more local basis."

This limited conception of the region has had an important impact on the kind of regional efforts that municipal officials seem willing to pursue. Inter-local coalitions are scaled down to contiguous localities. Inter-municipal associations, arranged to support municipalities with shared experiences and common problems, organize around geographic boundaries. By contrast, efforts at a scale that encompasses the Boston region as a whole are rarely attempted spontaneously—and not simply because it would be more difficult to coordinate with such a large number of jurisdictions. An official from Holliston explained that his town works with the 10 or 12 nearby towns but that there was little commonality with other towns in and around Boston. "A new mall in Newton wouldn't really affect us," he said.

A state effort to promote inter-local connections at the scale of the Boston region would, therefore, strike many local officials as an attempt to force them to share power with utter strangers, if not outright antagonists. To many, the Boston region seems no more connected to the interests of their municipality than the state itself. Reflective of this sentiment were the comments of an official from Reading, who argued that "the greater Boston region is too large to be manageable. Its problems are too diverse . . . . Appropriately sized and governed counties are great, but otherwise counties and other forms of regional governing bodies are bad. The Boston Regional Area is not the way to go. We've had some colossal failures with that." A respondent from Malden was even more blunt: "I couldn't support regional government at all . . . . Each community has its own unique set of circumstances and facts and issues. You need to be local on most issues. On the regional issues, you pick and choose which relationships you want to be involved with; we don't need an all encompassing regional government . . . . I don't care about traffic unless it impacts Malden."

Conflicts Between Home Rule and Regionalism

The lack of association with the Boston region as a whole is coupled with a strong sense among many of those we interviewed that having "home rule" meant local independence and autonomy. An Acton official explained that there is a "huge emphasis on self-reliance" in Massachusetts, and it is generally considered a "badge of honor to be independent of everybody else around you." Cooperation, by contrast, was described, even by some of its supporters, as disempowering. An administrator from Milford noted how regional cooperation was automatically equated with giving up control and power: "When you try to do something with another town . . . something on a regional basis . . . [t]hen all the bad connotations of politics come about because all these people want control. It's our natural instincts—towns and people hate to give up power."

To be sure, a few officials did say that increased accountability for regional concerns would make their municipalities better off. Those that perceived increased accountability in this more positive light commented on how it would allow municipalities to "improve . . . health insurance, schools, water and electricity infrastructure" (Beverly) without having to "plan around an arbitrary line" (Boxborough). Others were hopeful that municipalities have begun to move beyond a parochial attitude. As an official from Everett put it: "Cities were very competitive with each other on every level, from high school sports to going after grant dollars, doing projects, stealing business from each other. Since we've been here a few things have happened: cities have been very cooperative."

Yet even many of these supporters of regionalism were wary of losing more local power or having the state mandate cooperative arrangements. A counsel for several towns stated: "The towns are better off with more regionalism, but I wouldn't want to see a diminution in local government control of local issues. Local governments as such ought to be more involved in regional concerns." On this point, the perspective of the opponents of regional accountability was not that different from that of its supporters. Most of the negative reactions to regionalism were rooted in a fear that it would lead to more regulation and control on top of already existing state regulations. A respondent from Nahant asserted that there would be a "hue and cry" if the towns were ever told they must "do this and report back" to a regional form of government; it would thrust them back to 1984, creating a feeling of "big brother over them." He said that "towns should have the right not to cooperate if they did not want to." An Essex official similarly expressed his opinion that the town would be worse off if people in a community were told what to do by members of another community: "It is part of their culture and their history that they govern themselves. They don't want somebody who is not a member of the community making decisions about what they can and cannot do."

A significant number of respondents said that, regardless of what they themselves felt, increased regionalism would not work in Massachusetts. The primary impediment seemed to them to be the state's tradition of home rule. Regional cooperation "is hard to envision here given the tradition of home rule in the New England towns," as one official put it. "There is openness to cooperation within certain parameters, but also a concern for preserving local ideals." An administrator from Carlisle stated simply: "The idea of regional government flies in the face of home rule and local control." Regardless of the problems generated by the parochialism and competitive nature of localities, the general belief seemed to be that home rule and regional cooperation were at odds with one another.

Recognizing Inter-local Effects

A number of local officials we interviewed—sometimes in the very same interview in which they celebrated local independence—recognized the limitations of thinking about home rule in the way just described. They identified the external effects of decision making by their neighbors as a real threat to their own ability to respond to the needs of their residents. Many municipal officials referred to the same example: large-scale commercial developments in neighboring communities that threatened to create traffic congestion in their own. "You might have a major development going in and most of the traffic to access it will come in through the other community," a Winchester official explained. "But the one where it's located gets all the tax benefits and financial benefits. We often get into disputes about that. [Yet] it usually comes out without any cooperation."

This line of critique was levied against many different developments. A Westwood official disapproved of the proposed site for a regional mall in Norwood along the Westwood/Norwood border because "it had consequences for us but we wouldn't get any revenue from it." Another Westwood official added that, because "[Norwood] is much larger and more commercial . . . they have their own agenda. Their commercial areas often abut our residential areas and they will make decisions on their own without a lot of input from the town of Westwood. We have to keep an eye on things." A respondent from Peabody complained about the North Shore shopping center because "Peabody absorbs all the traffic and aggravation without direct benefit." An Arlington official expressed concerns about Belmont's and Cambridge's development in the Alewife area, stating:

> To us it looks like they are putting their developments on the outskirts of their community, which has already and will continue to flood Arlington with traffic. We can talk to them about regional planning and regional cooperation, but they won't talk. There is some property that we want to buy down by Alewife to do open space, whereas they are encouraging development to raise their tax base. So while they're saying that we should put in open space, they keep putting money into their pockets.

In a similar vein, administrators from Littleton and Acton complained about the large facility that Cisco is building in Boxborough. The Littleton official said that their town is turning to the courts to resolve the traffic problems the Cisco facility will bring in. The Acton official explained how, even though the town is upset by this move, it is indicative of the general structure of cooperation in Massachusetts: "Just to show the hypocrisy of the whole thing . . . they'll get a lot of tax revenue. . . [and] we'll bear a lot of the traffic burden. Obviously, we'd like to get them to regionally share the cost of the traffic, but if it was flipped, we wouldn't want to."

An official from Newton noted the same kind of problem—the real impact that extra-local decisions have on his own city—but was equally skeptical that much could be done about it through inter-local efforts. A sense of isolation and independence seemed to underlay his assessment:

> It's to the point where you really don't expect it. There are certain things you don't ask because it's so beyond what anyone would do. The idea, for example, that Boston would come to the City of Newton and say, "Please don't develop this tract of land because the traffic is going to have an adverse affect on downtown Boston." We're not going to do that, and I'm sure if we went to a community west of us and said, "Please don't develop this piece of land

because it's going to have a devastating effect on traffic on a couple of roads, or if you develop please consider a development bonus based on your tax revenue." Yeah, right. That's not going to happen either.

THE STATE'S ROLE IN REGIONALISM

The comments quoted above suggest that an attachment to home rule—understood as local independence or autonomy from other cities and towns in the metropolitan area—impedes regional thinking and coordination. Contrary to what many believe, however, municipal parochialism and competition are not inherent characteristics of Massachusetts life, resistant to all structural, political, or theoretical attempts to dislodge it. Current attitudes towards regionalism and its relationship to home rule are nurtured and reinforced by the legal structure of home rule. As city and town officials themselves know all too well, there is no home rule in Massachusetts in the sense of local independence and autonomy. The state has established a complex mix of grants of and limitations on local power. This mix of powers and disabilities creates the constrained environment within which municipal officials operate, and it plays a major role in shaping municipal officials' judgments about the kind of coordination with other localities that is possible or desirable. The obstacles to regionalism, therefore, are not simply a function of local preferences to go it alone. State-imposed limitations on home rule—like the ones we have already highlighted as well as additional ones we describe below—play a major role in inhibiting inter-municipal cooperative efforts in the Boston area.

Impacts of State-Induced Competition and Parochialism

The aspects of state law that foster parochialism and inter-local competition may not have been intended to limit inter-local agreements, but they are no less an impediment to them just because they are not readily visible. Consider the fact that, notwithstanding the occasional ambitious exception, inter-local agreements now tend to concern matters that the parties know, right from the start, would benefit their municipality. An administrator from Everett said: "[W]hen the agenda is something that serves every community, the cooperation is high." A spokesperson from Franklin added that the issues most conducive to cooperative arrangements were "things that are less political, where there's not a lot of risk." This kind of aversion to risk is, of course, a quite common disposition in both individuals and governments. But one reason for this cautious attitude is the fact that localities are so constrained in their powers. In this way, the state's limits on local power contribute to, rather than diminish, local parochialism and inter-local competition. They encourage municipalities to guard the limited power that they now possess from encroachment by other municipalities.

As we have seen, even though most municipalities are aware that the exercise of unrestrained land use powers by the region's municipalities undermines their own land use plans, they are usually adamant about preserving their ability to exercise the powers they have and dismissive of the idea that land use decisions could be made in concert. They regard home rule as the ability to protect their own capacity to impose external effects on other communities even if it means that others are allowed to impose external effects on them. A change in the legal structure that threatened local discretion to act in this way would be of concern precisely because it might threaten a current competitive advantage while leaving little room for local initiative. Even though there is a risk of coming out behind, there is felt to be some security in knowing the terms of battle and the scope of power (limited though it may be) that these terms permit localities to exercise.

Constraints on municipal revenue-raising and expenditures are an example of state-imposed restrictions that make local officials averse to entering into inter-local arrangements that might diminish their already limited power. Administrators tend to guard their revenues against the possibility of expropriation or reallocation knowing that they lack the power to raise revenue to make up for budget shortfalls. They are equally reluctant to consider cooperative arrangements involving expenditures because of the lingering risk that they may not come out ahead in the end or that they will be seen by voters to have been snookered by a competitor. So deep is the fear of improving the financial position of a neighbor, and thus undermining their own competitive standing, that some officials expressed concern that municipal judgments about benefits were determined by comparing a municipality's own benefits with those of the other participating municipalities rather than considering whether it was benefiting when measured against its previous, non-cooperating, position. In other words, municipalities were not inclined to engage in cooperative efforts if they perceived the other municipality was getting more out of the arrangement, even if they stood to benefit themselves. A Hamilton official said that the town is considering whether it should attempt to regionalize services. He called the situation a "hot issue" and noted that it "is controversial because there is a sense that one town may benefit more than others . . . . We are always working at balancing these perceptions. But we realize that if everyone is counting beans like that, then the only alternative is that both towns pay more."

How State Law Limits Inter-local Cooperation

Local parochialism and competition—and the aspects of state law that encourage such attitudes and behavior—play a large role in creating an environment in which few municipal officials believe that thinking regionally has taken hold. But so, too, do state-imposed limits that more directly constrain the exercise of local experimentation aimed at cooperation.

To be sure, the state does permit the kind of small-scale coordination between clusters, or pairs, of municipalities within the region that so many of those we interviewed held out as a model. The state has passed enabling legislation that allows municipalities to form inter-municipal organizations that facilitate the planning and operations of various services, and it has outlined a model structure within which these cooperative efforts may be realized. Municipalities may establish, among other institutions, regional water and sewer authorities, regional school districts, regional police and fire districts, regional transit authorities, and regional charter commissions for establishing regional councils of government.[3] A number of municipalities in the region reported that they take advantage of this opportunity, and many of them have experienced entry into such agreements as a way of asserting local control.

Among the most successful and uncontroversial cooperative arrangements that now exist in the region have been those aimed at saving money. "Where money is concerned," according to a Swampscott official, "there is always cooperation." Several municipalities, for example, participate in joint procurement arrangements. These arrangements allow municipalities to pool their resources and buying power in order to purchase goods or services at reduced costs. Almost all the municipal officials we interviewed agreed that this was the one area that has produced the most cooperation among localities. A respondent from Middleton, whose town participates in the north shore consortium and cooperative purchasing efforts, notes that "economies of scale are much greater if [municipalities] work together." These joint purchasing arrangements range from office supplies to health insurance, and they provide benefits without compromising local autonomy on other matters.

On occasion, inter-local contracting authority is also used to address seemingly intractable conflicts, such as the recurrent disputes over land use development by neighboring communities. Malden has been successful in using an inter-local agreement to coordinate a development project with other municipalities right from the start. "Telecom City," according to a Malden official, "is an example. The project involves Malden, Medford, and Everett. We have 200 acres of land for development, and we are hoping to develop those acres into a telecommunications center to create jobs. There are 100 acres in Everett, 50 in Malden, and 50 in Medford."[4]

There are, however, important limits on the kinds of agreements that localities are empowered to reach under their current state-granted authority. The agreements often require the approval of a state agency, and there are state-imposed limitations on how much municipal power these voluntarily formed subregional organizations can exercise. The agreement that resulted in the Telecom City venture, for example, was made only after the three cities filed home rule petitions obtaining power that they otherwise would have lacked. Several officials noted that state law sometimes makes addressing regional problems through voluntary and cooperative arrangements surprisingly difficult. "Things would be made better off . . . if it was made easier to regionalize in cases where cities and towns wish to regionalize. Currently such efforts are very difficult due to things like civil service laws, inequality of the school building assistance program, certain environmental laws, and other state mandates," an official from Saugus remarked. "If obstacles to regionalization were removed, communities would do so on their own. State government needs to get out of the way sometimes. Sometimes government should work from the bottom up rather than top-down."

One obstacle that the state places in the way of inter-local agreements is the requirement that, especially when towns are involved, a legal relationship between municipalities must be subject to higher degrees of bureaucratic oversight than contractual relationships with the private sector. A Weston official said that a town could make a contract with a private entity without specific town meeting approval as long as adequate funds have been appropriated. But, in order to establish a contractual relationship with other municipalities, towns must wait until approval has been granted at the next town meeting even if the contract was for a negligible monetary sum. The official described a time when he was working for the town of Needham. It had received a wood-grinder, worth a quarter of a million dollars, from the Department of Environmental Protection to be shared with the communities in the area. Needham wanted to establish a contractual relationship to allow the surrounding thirteen municipalities to rent the wood-grinder whenever they needed it for $5,000 a year. Because this required an inter-municipal contract, it had to wait until all thirteen communities had their next town meeting to approve this arrangement. After that, the arrangement was further delayed because Needham had to get special legislation from the state to establish a revolving fund so the money paid for the machine could be kept separate and used only for its servicing and maintenance. Although the agreement was finally put into place, the wood-grinder sat in Needham during this entire process and only Needham was able to use it. Had this piece of equipment belonged to a private company, the procedural limitations would not have been an issue.

Even establishing regional cooperation among municipalities for emergency services can be difficult. Although some officials were content with the agreements they had with neighboring municipalities requiring the sharing of emergency equipment and personnel, others noted that regional police and fire districts, regional dispatch systems, and the sharing of certain large-scale equipment are resisted by many municipalities. Officials from Medfield and Wakefield spoke specifically of the lack of cooperation on efforts to establish regional dispatch systems and regional police and fire departments. An official from Burlington said, "every town holds its own fire department 'sacrosanct.'" A spokesman for Boxborough told us that only one building in town required a five-story fire truck and, therefore, that sharing the truck with the town next door "seem[ed] like an obvious situation where we should cooperate." That town had such a truck, and Boxborough didn't, yet the arrangement never worked out. An official from Concord said that it seems "every town has a $700,000 ladder truck because we can't share. This is horribly inefficient." A representative from Weston gave a detailed account of how the town's efforts at establishing a regional dispatch system fared:

> [A] group of us got together and said this is a good chance to look at the way we dispatch our public safety services. We looked at combining fire and police dispatch, and civilian dispatch. And based on a model we'd seen in the Midwest, we said, "Why do all these small towns need to have their own dispatcher? Could we have regional dispatchers? Could Needham and Sherborn and Dover share, so all the calls would go to a regional dispatcher?" . . . Well, we worked on this for a year and a half, and in the end, the only communities that were left were Needham and Natick, who were willing to do it. To chiefs—for whatever reason, good or bad . . . the thought of giving up control of something like dispatching just panicked them. You would've thought we were attacking Mother Teresa. So one by one the communities dropped out.

As a number of respondents noted, there are personnel reasons—such as the desire of a long-serving fire official to become chief of his own department—that make such agreements difficult. Basic notions of municipal pride play a role as well. Yet state law also creates disincentives for forging such arrangements. "We were faced with the need to build a police and fire station, and it seemed like the right moment to reach out to other towns," a Hamilton official told us. "We had wooed Wenham on going joint on fire service. In fact, no other community around us wanted to regionalize with us on this issue because under the Mass General Law, a multi-town fire district results in financial dealings being less under the direct control of local town governments than if the towns had their own fire departments."

Other respondents pointed to the role that the Massachusetts Bay Transit Authority (MBTA) plays in frustrating inter-local transportation agreements. An official from Bedford explained that his town would like to establish a Route 128 corridor transportation system with other towns in the area "but right now everything is controlled by the MBTA, which is Boston-centric and basically operates the system as one big commuting system getting people into and out of Boston." He said that he had thought about the towns setting up a system on their own to shuttle people from town center to town center, but "the towns can't pay for it themselves because there's nowhere to get the money." A similar complaint was voiced by a respondent from Norfolk, who contended that the obstacle to such an inter-town transportation system was not simply a lack of funds but a lack of legal authority. "Norfolk doesn't want to build lots of roads and follow the '128 model' of dealing with development. They want to institute regional bus service to the commuter rail and perhaps in between suburbs to maintain the semi-rural identity. But the MBTA and the state prohibit this."

To some extent, the complaints voiced above underscore the complexity of thinking like a region. State laws that enable communities to establish regional school districts and similar regional institutions increase inter-local cooperation, but they simultaneously fragment the region as a whole. It is no surprise that so many of our respondents instinctively conceived of the "region" as the territory encompassing their contiguous neighbors. State law deems such small-scale areas "regions" for purposes of designating school districts, fire districts, and the like. This idea of the region is problematic, however, because job markets, housing markets, and commuting patterns actually encompass the larger area in which the 101 towns we examined are located. The more that small clusters of communities within the Boston region can design their own transportation networks, the more that a broader, region-wide transportation plan may be thwarted.

The Lack of State Mechanisms to Foster Regional Ties

It's not just that the state affirmatively creates a structure of home rule that creates incentives for localities to hunker down and look upon joint ventures as threatening propositions. Nor is it just that the state places limits on local powers to enter into inter-local agreements that make them unduly burdensome or even beyond local authority. Although the state is intimately involved with "local" concerns when it seeks to check selfish exercises of municipal power, it spends comparatively little effort in creating mechanisms through which localities might discover and assess the benefits of cooperating with one another. Aside from provisions authorizing small-scale cooperation that may arise spontaneously (discussed below), the state has not used its intervention into municipal affairs to create an atmosphere in which inter-local agreements might arise, let alone one in which a broader regional identification might take hold. Quite the contrary: the home rule petition process and state supervision of municipal entities tend to encourage vertical interactions with the state at the expense of horizontal relationships among municipalities.

Most town officials described the various organizations and associations to which they belonged, such as the Massachusetts Municipal Association or the Metropolitan Mayors Coalition, and they described them as important forums where regional issues were addressed. Weekly, biweekly, or monthly meetings of municipal officials break up the often isolated nature of municipal governance and exposed local officials to the experiences and issues facing other communities. Some who agreed that there was a lot of communication between individual communities felt, however, that there was too much "talk" and too little "action" to count as cooperation. Other than this structure for communication, a number of municipal officials acknowledged, there is little formal structure for cooperation among municipalities without relying on the state. The state has established one potential vehicle for such cooperation, the Metropolitan Area Planning Council. Established in 1963, the MAPC is comprised of representatives of 101 cities and towns in the metropolitan area. The MAPC has limited formal powers and none of our respondents identified it as providing the kind of structure that is needed. A Salem official said that "there needs to be a structure for cooperation and taking down of borders, at least around certain issues like schools, transportation, and joint purchasing." An official from Medway agreed, concluding that regional cooperation is low not because localities don't want it but because there is not a mechanism for enabling it. "There's just not any structure for towns to cooperate with one another on a formal basis," he said. "If more regionalization was encouraged by the state, it might be good."

In part for this reason, many municipalities now attempt to address their problems with their neighbors by seeking state intervention into their neighbors' affairs, or threatening to assert their own power in harmful ways, instead of finding common ground for collective action. A Boston official recounted how the city proposed a bill in the state legislature to assess penalties against municipalities that have not complied with the affordable housing requirements of Chapter 40B. Although the city was aware that the proposed bill would be rejected by the legislature, city officials thought that it would "tickle" the suburbs, encouraging them to contribute more effort on the problem of affordable housing. The concern of Boston about the need to provide more affordable housing—and the similar concern of the other communities who provide the majority of affordable housing in the region—is reasonable. Yet most municipalities, like Boston, see these problems as issues that can only be resolved by the state. They rarely consider the possibility that other municipalities may be able or willing to cooperate in resolving the issues without having to lobby the state for more statutory mandates. It's more likely that they would employ threats to compel other localities to come to the negotiating table. An official from Malden jokingly described how the city once threatened to turn all the roads leading in and out of a bordering development into one-way streets all moving in the same direction in order to compel its neighbor to discuss the development with them.

Some municipalities have been successful in rallying coalitions of support, such as the collection of communities that are working together to oppose the runway expansion at Logan International Airport. For the most part, however, regional support and cooperative efforts aimed at addressing long-standing problems have been ignored in favor of preserving the status quo or turning towards the state. According to a Wilmington official, it is "more important[], and realistic[] . . . [for] towns and cities . . . to improve their relationship with the state and establish a dialogue so that they have more of a voice in state decisions."

Options for Regionalism and Home Rule

To this point, we have described the state of home rule in Massachusetts as a matter of law and practice. We have found that local officials in the region believe they lack many of the legal powers they need. We have also found that, as much as local officials desire greater power, they recognize that there are substantial costs to pursuing a go-it-alone approach. Their own ability to meet the needs of their residents is powerfully affected by actions that occur beyond their borders. Finally, we have found that very few municipalities favor addressing these inter-local pressures through a new layer of governmental power at the regional level.

Rather than viewing this complex picture as a hopeless jumble of contradictions, we are inclined to see it as the basis for trying a new strategy for promoting regionalism. The fact that the state places so many limits on local power—and that these limits are experienced as significant by so many of the officials with whom we spoke—suggests to us that innovative approaches might be possible that would call into question the supposed conflict between home rule and regionalism. It is important to recognize, however, that any regional approach—no mater how innovative—depends on the state's willingness to assume an affirmative role to bring it about. Some of the local officials we interviewed asserted that regionalization would happen if only the state would "get out of the way." But it is not clear to us what it would mean for the state to "get out of the way." Local parochialism and inter-local competitiveness are realities. Indeed, the state, as the source of local power, has created the legal structure that fosters this parochialism and inter-local competitiveness. The question, then, cannot be what localities can do without the state. The question must be: how should the state go about promoting greater intra-regional coordination?

One possibility would be for the state to mandate regionalism from above. The Home Rule Amendment empowers the state to do just that:

> The general court shall have the power . . . to erect and constitute metropolitan and regional entities, embracing any two or more cities or towns, or established with other than existing city and town boundaries, for any general or special public purpose or purposes, and to grant to these entities such powers, privileges and immunities as the general court shall deem necessary or expedient for the regulation and government thereof.[5]

This solution strikes us as unrealistic and unproductive. The virtually uniformly hostile responses that such an idea provoked among our respondents underscores the resistance that it would face. This is the type of regionalism that can accurately be described as one more state mandate—the type of regionalism that inspired so many officials to embrace local independence and autonomy as an alternative ideal. Another reason to be skeptical about this type of regionalism is that centralization—in the form of state power—has too often been the source of, rather than a solution to, the problems generated by the coexistence of so many cities and towns in the Boston metropolitan area.

Another possibility would be to provide state aid to encourage local governments to act on a more regional basis. Such a solution is also problematic. It would require substantial outlays of new money that is not now available and is unlikely to be available anytime soon. Besides, existing state grants-in-aid already have a distorting effect on municipal governments, leading them to devise programs to obtain sorely needed revenue from the state when alternative policies might be better. And, of course, if the regionalism string were attached to existing dollars, few municipalities would experience the state as offering them a meaningful choice. The distinction between a grant-with-strings and an outright mandate is not one that impressed many of the officials we interviewed.

A better alternative, we suggest, is to promote regionalism by responding seriously to the widespread sentiment that the state has unduly limited home rule. The idea would be for the state to enhance local power—and relax existing limitations on that power—as a carrot to induce greater regionalism. In this way, the state would help overcome the sense of opposition between home rule and regionalism that so many municipal officials we interviewed took as a given. To make this proposal more concrete, we offer some examples from the three substantive areas discussed in earlier sections of this report: revenues, land use, and education. What we offer here is not a menu for legislative reform. Our goal in presenting these ideas is much more limited: our proposals are designed to demonstrate that increasing local power and regionalism can go hand-in-hand.

Virtually every municipal official we interviewed emphasized the lack of local power with respect to fiscal matters. The limits on municipal power range from the Home Rule Amendment's exclusion of the power to tax to Proposition 2½'s constraints on property taxing authority to the detailed state supervision that occurs at every stage of the local revenue-raising process. These constraints are made even more onerous by the state's substantial role in mandating local spending. The result, as we have seen, is a disconnect between revenues and expenditures that prevents local budgeting from being an exercise in expressing municipal will. Municipal officials also recognized that the state's limits on taxation, and its mandates to spend, are not the only constraints on local fiscal control. They were quick to point out that their city's or town's fiscal health was in large part determined by its success in battling neighbors for commercial and residential development. The wealth of the residents a municipality attracts or loses—and the costs that accompany either move—plays a large role in determining municipal fiscal capacity.

To address these two limitations on local fiscal authority, the state must do more than simply loosen restrictions on local revenue-raising power. It needs to expand local control in a way that will not exacerbate the inter-local battle for taxable property. One way to do this would be to tie grants of greater local tax authority to regionalization. The possibilities are numerous. The state could grant a group of localities a limited power to impose a sales tax as long as they agreed to share the new revenue. Alternatively, the state could offer to reimburse localities (in whole or in part) for the lost revenue generated by state-owned, tax-exempt property as long as the municipalities collectively submitted to the state a plan detailing where such new state properties should be located. In this way, the region's cities would have an incentive to formulate joint plans about the location of new state buildings rather than to try to exclude or court the property based on a self-interested assessment of whether it would attract more net revenue. Yet another example would involve neither raising locally imposed taxes nor increasing state payments. The state could enhance municipal authority to offer tax abatements to attract development as long as the locality agreed to share a portion of the generated revenue with neighboring localities. Any of these ideas—and many more like them—would increase the incentives for coordination within the region without increasing state control over local power. Regionalism would become a byproduct of state efforts to enhance local power rather than to limit it.

Unlike the situation with regard to revenue, municipalities have significant control over land use and want to keep it. The officials we interviewed repeatedly pointed to zoning as an area in which the state had ceded significant discretion. Yet, as these respondents also noted, the state imposes a broad range of limitations on the land use powers that localities may assert. Many of these limitations are included in the state statutes that delegate the zoning power. One particularly noteworthy example is the generous granting of vested rights that state law now affords property owners. The vested rights provisions of Chapter 40A make changes in local land use planning difficult and, sometimes, even counterproductive. To respond to this problem, the state could relax this requirement in the name of enhancing local home rule. But this solution would not fully respond to the concerns localities have about their land use authority because they are also limited in what they can do by the relative position of their neighbors. Land use choices may be driven by a felt need to win out in the competition for new developments or affected by development policies pursued across the border.

In order to think about home rule and regionalism as complements, the state could address both types of limitations on local land use powers without exacerbating inter-local battles. It could relax the early vesting rules only for cities and towns that enter into regional land use planning agreements. In this way, municipal power to manage growth would increase as cities and towns agreed to work together to devise a greater-than-local land use strategy. Cooperation would make planning strategies possible that now are effectively foreclosed.

Another possible state land use approach would deal with current affordable housing regulation. There has been much talk in recent months of regionalizing Chapter 40B's affordable housing requirement. Under this approach, regions rather than individual towns would be responsible for meeting the 10 percent requirement that state law establishes. Some respondents cited this potential change as an example of why regionalism worries them. They explained that their town had already taken efforts to meet the 10 percent goal while neighboring communities had not. If they were lumped together into a region for purposes of Chapter 40B, they feared, they would be denied the benefits that their prior efforts merited. Whether or not regionalizing Chapter 40B is a good idea, too little attention has been given in the discussion about reforming Chapter 40B to the need to expand local power to promote and preserve affordable housing. As our report shows, the general grant of home rule power leaves local governments without an adequate set of tools for making affordable housing available to their residents. Part of what the towns lack under the current Chapter 40B regime, in other words, is the legal authority to promote its purposes. Expanding home rule power to adopt inclusionary zoning ordinances or other means of stimulating the building of affordable housing can promote the regional goal of more equitable distribution of affordable housing.

Our final example concerns education. As we have noted, regional school districts can be established under Massachusetts law. They can be created by the agreement of two or more municipalities upon the recommendation of a regional school district planning board. The schools are then run by a regional school committee that exercises the power of a local school committee. Regional school districts often save municipalities money, but establishing them is difficult. In explaining the obstacles to their creation, municipal officials focused on the disconnect between the municipalities and the regional schools. Echoing the criticism that other localities had of school committees generally, they complained that the involvement of municipalities participating in a regional school district was limited to approving the budget and paying their portion of the bill. A Pembroke official, whose town recently withdrew from a regional school district, stated that "when school systems are regional, the town merely gets a bill and pays it. When the system is taken local, as Pembroke is doing, [we] will be more cognizant of the affairs of the school and be more proactive. Local involvement will be more than footing a state-mandated bill." Conflicts also arise over the formula used to assess the participating localities. Tensions particularly arise if one municipality—or even worse, a coalition of municipalities—perceives another municipality as getting a better deal because of its class-based character.

Perhaps municipal administrators are more inclined to participate in the affairs of their own local school committee. Yet there is little evidence that they actually are more involved with local school committees than with regional school committees. As we have pointed out, legally and structurally, local school committees and regional school committees are both kept distant from municipal governments. It is possible, then, that the feared disconnect between municipalities and regional school districts has less to do with the organization of regional school districts than with the perception of a loss of "home rule" when schools are marked off as "regional" as opposed to "local." To make regional school districts more attractive, municipal governments could be given a greater role over regional schools than they now possess over local schools. They could be given such a greater role in two ways. Their power to formulate school policy could be increased. And they could also have more influence on the regional school budget than individual cities and towns now have over local school budgets.

All of the ideas just presented—on revenue, land-use and education—envision permitting regional agreements signed by only a few municipalities, rather than covering the region as a whole. Given the widespread current preference for these sub-regions as the definition of the relevant region, this may well be a way for any new form of regionalism to begin in the Boston area. But, as we have already noted, this kind of sub-regional thinking threatens to fracture the region as a whole at the very time that it creates greater-than-local approaches to common problems. To counter this tendency, any of the proposals just made could be structured so that greater authority would be transferred to municipalities depending on the number of cities and towns willing to enter into the regional undertaking. With each new city or town added, the control of the municipal governments could be increased relative to the state. Once again, this way of inducing regionalism would expand home rule power rather than reduce it.

Even if implemented, none of the proposals just sketched would fully address any, let alone all, of the problems facing the Boston region set forth at the outset of this report. The problems of housing affordability, sprawl, traffic congestion, and environmental degradation that stem from the current way localities exercise their power cannot easily be overcome. Moreover, as we have already emphasized, we have not made these suggestions in the expectation that they would become a concrete agenda for reform. We sought instead to propose a number of ideas that might enable readers to revise the standard notion that regionalism of necessity erodes home rule. All of the proposals—and many more like them—would restructure home rule in Massachusetts in a way that empowered localities rather than weakened them. Indeed, they would remove limits on local power that now restrict Massachusetts municipalities more than those of other states. At the same time, they would create incentives for the region's municipalities to see the benefits of thinking regionally beyond the easy, non-political matters that now bring them together. Over time, this new conception of regionalism—in whatever concrete form it is adopted—might begin to instill a regional sensibility that at present does not exist.

Proposals such as ours do not seek to resurrect home rule in the sense of "local autonomy." To our way of thinking, that is what makes them attractive. The "local autonomy" definition of home rule now stifles the discussion of regionalism. And it is the principal justification for the kinds of state control over local decision making outlined in this report. As this report suggests, "home rule" does not now enable the cities and towns of Massachusetts to exercise local autonomy. Instead, home rule is a complex, deeply contested concept. Our hope is that this report will help readers think creatively about what home rule is and what they want it to be.

Appendix A

GREATER BOSTON

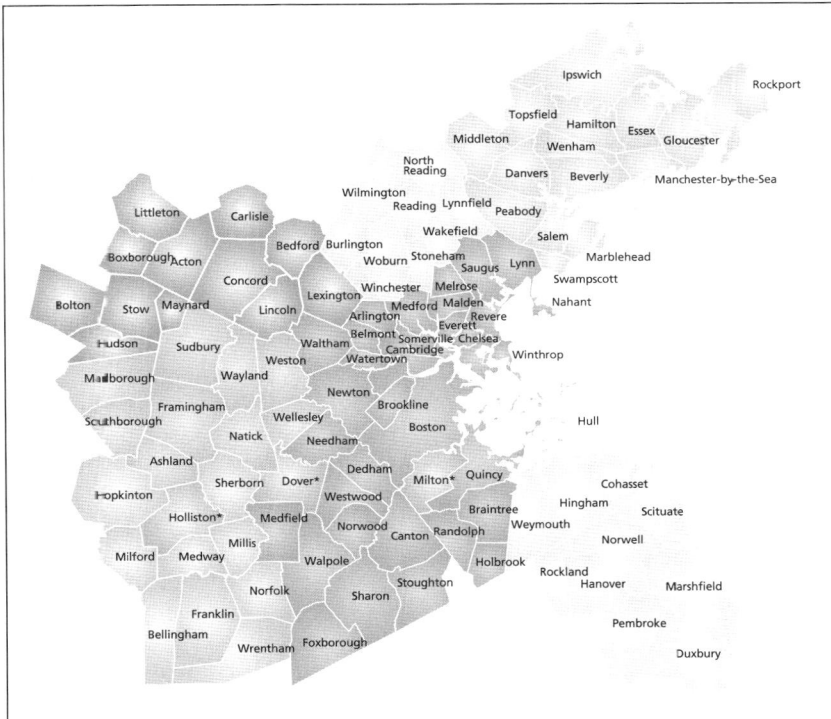

The Greater Boston area includes 101 cities and towns extending west to Route 495 under the Metropolitan Area Planning Council's jurisdiction (below). The U.S. Census includes more communities under the Standard Metropolitan Area (SMA) and Standard Metropolitan Statistical Area (SMSA).

Appendix B

HOME RULE PROJECT PARTICIPANTS

Tom Brown

Jerome Chou

Charles Imohiosen

Lisa Johnson

Najeeb Khoury

Dominick Lanza

Mary Catherine Martin

Jeremy McClane

Rebecca Onie

Paul Schoenhard

Justin Tichauer

Geoffrey Upton

John Verdi

David Ware

Special thanks go to David J. Harding, a doctoral candidate in Sociology and Social Policy at Harvard University, who helped us in formulating questions for our interviews and numerous other aspects of this report.

Appendix C

LIST OF THE SIXTY MUNICIPALITIES INTERVIEWED FOR THIS REPORT

Acton	Holliston	Norfolk
Arlington	Hopkinton	Norwood
Ashland	Hull	Peabody
Bedford	Lexington	Pembroke
Beverly	Lincoln	Reading
Boston	Littleton	Salem
Boxborough	Lynn	Saugus
Burlington	Malden	Sharon
Cambridge	Marblehead	Sherborn
Carlisle	Medfield	Southborough
Cohasset	Medford	Swampscott
Concord	Medway	Topsfield
Dover	Melrose	Wakefield
Duxbury	Middleton	Walpole
Essex	Milford	Wellesley
Everett	Millis	Wenham
Foxborough	Milton	Weston
Franklin	Nahant	Westwood
Gloucester	Natick	Wilmington
Hamilton	Newton	Winchester

Appendix D

ARTICLE LXXXIX
(Home Rule Amendment)

Article II of the Articles of Amendment to the Constitution of the Commonwealth, as amended by Article LXX of said Articles of Amendment, is hereby annulled and the following is adopted in place thereof:

ARTICLE II. SECTION 1. RIGHT OF LOCAL SELF-GOVERNMENT.   It is the intention of this article to reaffirm the customary and traditional liberties of the people with respect to the conduct of their local government, and to grant and confirm to the people of every city and town the right of self-government in local matters, subject to the provisions of this article and to such standards and requirements as the general court may establish by law in accordance with the provisions of this article.

SECTION 2. LOCAL POWER TO ADOPT, REVISE OR AMEND CHARTERS.   Any city or town shall have the power to adopt or revise a charter or to amend its existing charter through the procedures set forth in sections three and four. The provisions of any adopted or revised charter or any charter amendment shall not be inconsistent with the constitution or any laws enacted by the general court in conformity with the powers reserved to the general court by section eight.

No town of fewer than twelve thousand inhabitants shall adopt a city form of government, and no town of fewer than six thousand inhabitants shall adopt a form of government providing for a town meeting limited to such inhabitants of the town as may be elected to meet, deliberate, act and vote in the exercise of the corporate powers of the town.

SECTION 3. PROCEDURE FOR ADOPTION OR REVISION OF A CHARTER BY A CITY OR TOWN.   Every city and town shall have the power to adopt or revise a charter in the following manner: A petition for the adoption or revision of a charter shall be signed by at least fifteen per cent of the number of legal voters residing in such city or town at the preceding state election. Whenever such a petition is filed with the board of registrars of voters of any city or town, the board shall within ten days of its receipt determine the sufficiency and validity of the signatures and certify the results to the city council of the city or board of selectmen of the town, as the case may be. As used in this section, the phrase "board of registrars of voters" shall include any local authority of different designation which performs the duties of such registrars, and the phrase "city council of the city or board of selectmen of the town" shall include local authorities of different designation performing the duties of such council or board. Objections to the sufficiency and validity of the signatures on any such petition as certified by the board of registrars of voters shall be made in the same manner as provided by law for objections to nominations for city or town offices, as the case may be.

Within thirty days of receipt of certification of the board of registrars of voters that a petition contains sufficient valid signatures, the city council of the city or board of selectmen of the town shall by order provide for submitting to the voters of the city or town the question of adopting or revising a charter, and for the nomination and election of a charter commission.

If the city or town has not previously adopted a charter pursuant to this section, the question submitted to the voters shall be: "Shall a commission be elected to frame a charter for (name of city or town)?" If the city or town has previously adopted a charter pursuant to this section, the question submitted to the voters shall be: "Shall a commission be elected to revise the charter of (name of city or town)?"

The charter commission shall consist of nine voters of the city or town, who shall be elected at large without party or political designation at the city or town election next held at least sixty days after the order of the city council of the city or board of selectmen of the town. The names of candidates for such commission shall be listed alphabetically on the ballot used at such election. Each voter may vote for nine candidates.

The vote on the question submitted and the election of the charter commission shall take place at the same time. If the vote on the question submitted is in the affirmative, the nine candidates receiving the highest number of votes shall be declared elected.

Within [ten months] after the election of the members of the charter commission, said commission shall submit the charter or revised charter to the city council of the city or the board of selectmen of the town, and such council or board shall provide for publication of the charter and for its submission to the voters of the city or town at the next city or town election held at least two months after such submission by the charter commission. If the charter or revised charter is approved by a majority of the voters of the city or town voting thereon, it shall become effective upon the date fixed in the charter. [See Amendments, Art. CXIII.]

SECTION 4. PROCEDURE FOR AMENDMENT OF A CHARTER BY A CITY OR TOWN.

Every city and town shall have the power to amend its charter in the following manner: The legislative body of a city or town may, by a two-thirds vote, propose amendments to the charter of the city or town; provided, that [1] amendments of a city charter may be proposed only with the concurrence of the mayor in every city that has a mayor, and [2] any change in a charter relating in any way to the composition, mode of election or appointment, or terms of office of the legislative body, the mayor or city manager or the board of selectmen or town manager shall be made only by the procedure of charter revision set forth in section three.

All proposed charter amendments shall be published and submitted for approval in the same manner as provided for adoption or revision of a charter.

Section 5. Recording of Charters and Charter Amendments.   Duplicate certificates shall be prepared setting forth any charter that has been adopted or revised and any charter amendments approved, and shall be signed by the city or town clerk. One such certificate shall be deposited in the office of the secretary of the commonwealth and the other shall be recorded in the records of the city or town and deposited among its archives. All courts may take judicial notice of charters and charter amendments of cities and towns.

Section 6. Governmental Powers of Cities and Towns.   Any city or town may, by the adoption, amendment, or repeal of local ordinances or by-laws, exercise any power or function which the general court has power to confer upon it, which is not inconsistent with the constitution or laws enacted by the general court in conformity with powers reserved to the general court in conformity with powers reserved to the general court by section eight, and which is not denied, either expressly or by clear implication, to the city or town by its charter. This section shall apply to every city and town, whether or not it has adopted a charter pursuant to section three.

Section 7. Limitations on Local Powers.   Nothing in this article shall be deemed to grant to any city or town the power to (1) regulate elections other than those prescribed by sections three and four; (2) to levy, assess and collect taxes; (3) to borrow money or pledge the credit of the city or town; (4) to dispose of park land; (5) to enact private or civil law governing civil relationships except as an incident to an exercise of an independent municipal power; or (6) to define and provide for the punishment of a felony or to impose imprisonment as a punishment for any violation of law; provided, however, that the foregoing enumerated powers may be granted by the general court in conformity with the constitution and with the powers reserved to the general court by section eight; nor shall the provisions of this article be deemed to diminish the powers of the judicial department of the commonwealth.

SECTION 8. POWERS OF THE GENERAL COURT. The general court shall have the power to act in relation to cities and towns, but only by general laws which apply alike to all cities or to all towns, or to all cities and towns, or to a class of not fewer than two, and by special laws enacted (1) on petition filed or approved by the voters of a city or town, or the mayor and city council, or other legislative body, of a city, or the town meeting of a town, with respect to a law relating to that city or town; (2) by a two-thirds vote of each branch of the general court following a recommendation by the governor; (3) to erect and constitute metropolitan or regional entities, embracing any two or more cities or towns or cities and towns, or established with other than existing city or town boundaries, for any general or special public purpose or purposes, and to grant to these entities such powers, privileges and immunities as the general court shall deem necessary or expedient for the regulation and government thereof; or (4) solely for the incorporation or dissolution of cities or towns as corporate entities, alteration of city or town boundaries, and merger or consolidation of cities and towns, or any of these matters.

Subject to the foregoing requirements, the general court may provide optional plans of city or town organization and government under which an optional plan may be adopted or abandoned by majority vote of the voters of the city or town voting thereon at a city or town election; provided, that no town of fewer than twelve thousand inhabitants may be authorized to adopt a city form of government, and no town of fewer than six thousand inhabitants may be authorized to adopt a form of town government providing for town meeting limited to such inhabitants of the town as may be elected to meet, deliberate, act and vote in the exercise of the corporate powers of the town.

This section shall apply to every city and town whether or not it has adopted a charter pursuant to section three.

SECTION 9. EXISTING SPECIAL LAWS. All special laws relating to individual cities or towns shall remain in effect and have the force of an existing city or town charter, but shall be subject to amendment or repeal through the adoption, revision or amendment of a charter by a city or town in accordance with the provisions of sections three and four and shall be subject to amendment or repeal by laws enacted by the general court in conformity with the powers reserved to the general court by section eight.

ABOUT THE AUTHORS

David Barron is an Assistant Professor of Law at Harvard Law School, where he teaches local government law. He is the author, among other works, of "Reclaiming Home Rule," which appeared in the June 2003 issue of the *Harvard Law Review*. He is the co-author, with Gerald Frug and Richard T. Ford, of a casebook on the subject, *Local Government Law* (West Publishing Company, 2001, third edition), and recently served as chair of the State and Local Government Section of the American Association of Law Schools. He is a former law clerk to Justice John Paul Stevens of the United States Supreme Court and to Judge Stephen Reinhardt of the United States Court of Appeals for the Ninth Circuit.

Gerald Frug is the Louis D. Brandeis Professor of Law at Harvard Law School. Educated at the University of California at Berkeley and Harvard Law School, he worked as a Special Assistant to the Chairman of the Equal Employment Opportunity Commission, in Washington, D.C., and as Health Services Administrator of the City of New York, before he began teaching in 1974 at the University of Pennsylvania Law School. He joined the Harvard faculty in 1981. He is the author, among other works, of *City Making: Building Communities Without Building Walls* (Princeton University Press, 1999). He is coauthor, with David Barron and Richard T. Ford, of the casebook *Local Government Law* (West Publishing Company, 2001, third edition).

Rick Su is a third year law student at Harvard Law School and an Articles Editor for the *Harvard Law Review*. He received his B.A. from Dartmouth College. After graduating from Law School in 2004, he will be clerking for Judge Stephen Reinhardt of the United States Court of Appeals for the Ninth Circuit.

NOTES

CHAPTER 1

1. Mass. Const. art. LXXXIX (amended 1966) (amending Mass. Const. amend. art. II, § 2).
2. **Mass. Gen. Laws** ch. 43B (2003).
3. John W. Lemega, *State and Municipal Government: Home Rule*, in **1967 Annual Survey of Massachusetts Law**, § 16.2, at 264 (quoting Governor Volpe). See also Bloom v. City of Worcester, 363 Mass. 136, 143, 293 N.E.2d 268, 273 (1973) (describing the history of the Home Rule Amendment).
4. Mass. Const. art. LXXXIX, § 1.
5. State law prohibits any municipality with less than 12,000 residents from classifying itself as a city. *Id.* at § 2. It also prohibits any municipality with less than 6,000 residents from using the representative town meeting form of local government, in which the town meeting acts through representatives elected by town residents. *Id.*
6. The issue is not entirely free of complication. Although Massachusetts law specifically states that "by-laws" require the approval of the Attorney General, **Mass. Gen. Laws** ch.40, § 32 (2003), the Massachusetts Supreme Judicial Court explained that this statute was equally applicable to city ordinances. *See Forbes v. Woburn*, 306 Mass. 67, 69, 27 N.E.2d 733, 734 (1940) (noting that "towns" and "by-laws" are to be treated synonymously with "city" and "ordinances" respectively "unless such construction would be repugnant to the provision of any act, especially relating to such cities or districts."); *see also* **Mass. Gen. Laws** ch. 40, § 1 (2003) ("Except as otherwise expressly provided . . . all laws relative to towns shall apply to cities."); **Mass. Gen. Laws** ch. 4, § 7(22) ("'Ordinance', as applied to cities, shall be synonymous with by-law."). Nevertheless, the court found that Woburn, the city in question, was not bound by the approval requirement for two reasons. First, the court noted that a separate provision of the general laws granting mayors veto power over ordinances states that if there is no objection to an ordinance by the mayor within ten days, or if the veto is overturned by a two-thirds vote of the local legislative authority, then the ordinance "shall be in force." *See Forbes*, 306 Mass. at 71–72 (quoting **Mass. Gen. Laws** ch. 39, § 4). The court noted that the subsequent statute regarding the mayoral veto power impliedly did away with the Attorney General approval requirement since there is no time for an approval if the ordinance is "in force" immediately upon the absence of a veto within ten days or the veto being overturned. *Id.* Second, the court found that city charters adopted by almost all cities adopt, alter, or reject the veto power provision of section 4 of chapter 39 for ordinances passed by a single legislative body. *See id.* at 71–73. And in doing so, Woburn, along with possibly all other cities that took such action in their charters, also dispensed with the Attorney General approval requirement by indirectly stating when laws would come into effect and foreclosing the opportunity for an approval by the state official. Although the court explained that their "review of legislation shows that it is impossible, without examining every city charter, to be sure that there is no city to which" the Attorney General approval requirement is

applicable, analysis indicates that this may indeed be the case. *Id.* at 74.

The court's decision in 1940 reflected the legal structure then in place. Since city charters at that time were all special legislative acts passed by the state, it made sense to conclude that provisions in a charter could trump requirements set forth in a general state statute. Nevertheless, considering that, under the Home Rule Amendment, charters can be adopted locally without state participation, it is not clear whether cities can still include language in their charter to avoid the approval requirement of chapter 40, section 32. Indeed, it can be argued that any home rule charter that includes language similar to that which exempted Woburn from the approval requirement would be invalid for conflicting with existing state law, which means that existing state law would have to prevail. *See* Home Rule Procedures Act, **Mass. Gen. Laws** ch. 43B, § 9(b) (requiring the Attorney General to file a report documenting any conflicts between the Charter and the state constitution or existing state law).

7. **Mass. Gen. Laws** ch. 43. The sections in this chapter describe six model city governments that can be adopted—labeled "A" through "F." The Home Rule Procedures Act places an effective "freeze" on the adoption of these model governments according to the procedures outlined in chapter 43 after 1966. *See* Home Rule Procedures Act, **Mass. Gen. Laws** ch.43B, § 18.

8. Massachusetts Municipal Association, *Ask the MMA*, at http://mma.org/local_government/ask_mma/change_government.html (last visited November, 6, 2001) and copy on file with authors.

9. The Home Rule Charter does not eliminate a locality's ability to petition the state legislature for a special act to accomplish the same ends. In *Bd. of Selectmen of Braintree v. Town Clerk of Braintree*, the court ruled that there was no evidence to indicate that section 4 of the Home Rule Amendment, which outlines the charter amendment procedure, is a limitation on, or exception to, a municipality's power to petition the general court for the same result through the state legislature as outlined in section 8. 370 Mass. 114, 117–18, 345 N.E.2d 699, 701 (1976). Indeed, the Home Rule Amendment reserves for the state the power to pass acts "for the incorporation or dissolution of cities and towns as corporate entities." Home Rule Amendment, Mass. Const. art. LXXXIX, § 8.

10. Sections 2, 3, and 4 of the Home Rule Amendment, along with the Home Rule Procedures Act, outline the requirements for adopting, revising, or amending a home rule charter. *See* Home Rule Amendment, Mass. Const. art. LXXXIX, §§ 2–4; Home Rule Procedures Act, **Mass. Gen. Laws** ch. 43B (2003). Any municipality can adopt a home rule charter by first having fifteen percent of its registered voters sign a petition putting the question of electing a charter commission on the ballot. *See* Home Rule Procedures Act, **Mass. Gen. Laws** ch. 43B, § 3. If the charter commission is approved, it will then be responsible for drafting a new charter, which will be voted upon again by the electorate. The only role the state plays in this process is a legal review of the new charter by the state Attorney General to make sure that there is no conflict with existing state law. *Id.* at § 10(c). If the charter is approved, it is recorded and effective on the date specified in the charter.

11. *See* Massachusetts Department of Housing and Community Development, *Home Rule Amendment and the Home Rule Procedures Act—Summary*, 12 (2000), at http://www.state.ma.us/dhcd/publications/hrapsc.pdf (last visited August 21, 2003) [Hereinafter DHCD Home Rule Summary].

12. *See id.*
13. *See id.* at 7.
14. *See id.* at 1.
15. *Id.* at 12.
16. *See* Home Rule Amendment, Mass. Const. art. LXXXIX, § 3 ("The vote on the question [of whether to adopt or amend a Home Rule Charter] and the election of the charter commission shall take place at the same time. If the vote on the question submitted is in the affirmative, the nine candidates receiving the highest number of votes shall be declared elected.").
17. *See* DHCD Home Rule Summary, *supra* note **Error! Bookmark not defined.**, at 12.
18. *See* Home Rule Procedures Act, **Mass. Gen. Laws** ch. 43B, § 8(a)
19. *See id.* at § 9(c); *see also* Home Rule Amendment, Mass. Const. art. LXXXIX, § 3.
20. Once the final report for the adoption of revision of a charter is submitted by the charter commission, the question of whether to adopt the proposed charter is "submitted to the voters as a single question unless the charter commission provides for the separate submission of proposed revisions." Home Rule Procedures Act, **Mass. Gen. Laws** ch. 43B, § 11. Therefore, even though multiple proposals may be presented to the electorate, whether there are alternatives at all, or what forms those alternatives take, are decided entirely and independently by the charter commission. Furthermore, if the charter commission recommends that a home rule charter not be adopted or revised, then the process is also terminated without any opportunity for the municipal government or the voters to intervene. *See id.* ("[A] charter commission report which does not recommend the adoption or revision of a charter shall not be submitted to the voters.").
21. A charter proposal that has been denied by the electorate, but managed to receive thirty-five percent of the affirmative vote, can be resubmitted through a petition by the voters. *See id.* at §12A. Nevertheless, there is no authority in this section that allows any party to alter or amend the charter proposal for resubmission. The only changes that can be made are to the dates in the original charter proposal. *Id.*
22. *See* DHCD Home Rule Summary, *supra* note 10, at 7. The municipalities in the Boston region that have received special act charters after the passage of the Home Rule Amendment are Burlington, Duxbury, Framingham, Hull, Needham, Lexington, Stoneham, and Weymouth. *See id.*
23. Indeed, some municipalities with home rule charters continue to petition for special acts to amend their charter even though they have the power to change it locally. For example, the town of Acton has a home rule charter, which allows it to amend its charter to change the position of police chief to an appointed position. *See* Mass Const. amend. art. 2, § 4 (describing the procedure for amending a city or town charter). Municipalities in general are also enabled to do the same thing through a local referendum according to the Massachusetts General Laws. *See* **Mass. Gen. Laws** ch. 41, § 1B (2003). Nonetheless, Acton petitioned for and received a special legislation to convert the police chief position to an appointed office in 1998. It is not entirely clear why it petitioned for special legislation to enact this amendment, but there are two possible reasons. First, the police chief position in Acton was actually governed by previous special act legislation passed in 1938. The Home Rule Procedures Act does allow municipalities to amend or repeal special act legislation affecting only their municipality, but only if the special act legislation does not state otherwise and was enacted subsequent to the passage of the Home Rule

Amendment. *See* Home Rule Procedures Act, **Mass. Gen. Laws** ch. 43B, § 19. Since the special act legislation was passed prior to the Home Rule Amendment, arguably only another act of special legislation could alter it. Indeed, the specific language of the 1998 Acton special legislation simply stated that it repealed a previous act. Second, even if the special legislation could have been altered through the process outlined in the Home Rule Procedures Act or pursuant to the more specific authority granted by Chapter 41, § 1B of the general laws, both of those provisions require referendum approval, which is arguably more time- and resources-consuming than simply asking for a stamp of approval by the state, especially when the proposed change is relatively minor.

24. *See, e.g.,* **Mass. Gen. Laws** ch. 41, § 1B (allowing all towns to change certain elected positions to appointed positions through referendum); **Mass. Gen. Laws** ch. 41, § 21 (allowing all towns to either allow their selectmen to act as certain officers or empower them to appoint those positions through referendum).

25. *See* Home Rule Procedures Act, **Mass. Gen. Laws** ch. 43B, § 11 ("Upon submission of the final report of a charter commission under section nine, the city council or board of selectmen shall order the proposed charter or charter revision to be submitted to the voters . . . ."); *see also* Massachusetts Department of Housing and Community Development, The Home Rule Amendment and The Home Rule Procedures Act 4 (2001) ("The city council or board of selectmen upon receipt of the final charter commission report *must* order the charter proposal or charter revision to appear on the ballot . . . ." (emphasis in original)).

26. *See* Home Rule Procedures Act, **Mass. Gen. Laws** ch. 43B, § 10(c) ("If the attorney general reports that the proposed amendment conflicts with the constitution or laws of the commonwealth, the order proposing such amendment shall not take effect . . . .").

27. *See Beard v. Town of Salisbury*, 378 Mass. 435, 441, 392 N.E.2d 832, 836 (1979).

28. *Powers v. Secretary of Administration*, 412 Mass. 119, 129, 587 N.E.2d 744, 750 (1992).

29. *Id.* (citing *Opinion of the Justices*, 368 Mass. 849, 854, 332 N.E.2d 896 (1975)).

30. *See Boston Gas Company v. City of Somerville*, 420 Mass. 702, 704–05, 652 N.E.2d 132, 134 (1995) (finding state regulation on manufacture and sale of gas and electricity by public utilities to be so comprehensive as to preempt localities from regulating in this area).

31. *See Town of Wendell v. Attorney General*, 394 Mass. 518, 476 N.E.2d 585 (1985).

32. **Mass. Gen. Laws** ch. 40C ("Historical Districts").

33. **Mass. Gen. Laws** ch. 40A ("Zoning").

34. *See* Home Rule Amendment, Mass. Const. art. LXXXIX, § 8. Without the local government's consent, the state can pass special legislation by a two-thirds vote following a recommendation by the governor. *Id.*

35. *See Belin v. Secretary of the Commonwealth*, 362 Mass. 530, 534–35, 288 N.E.2d 287, 289 (1972) (holding legislation affecting municipalities with proportional representation voting void because Cambridge was the only municipality that fits that classification).

36. *See, e.g.,* 2003 Mass. Acts 10 (special legislation removing the town of Oak Bluffs from the Martha's Vineyard commission upon ballot approval by the voters); 2002 Mass. Acts 20 (special legislation amending charter to establish a director of finance

in Dedham, requiring ballot approval by the electorate); 2002 Mass. Acts 331 (special legislation expanding the Board of Selectmen in Canton requiring ballot approval).

CHAPTER 2

1. Property taxes are consistently the single largest contributor to a locality's revenues. In 2001 property taxes accounted for 49.64 percent of the total revenue of all Massachusetts municipalities. *See* Department of Revenue, Division of Local Services, *FY01 Municipal Revenue Components*, **City and Town,** May 2001, at 3. State aid and other local receipts trailed behind at 27.88 percent and 17.26 percent respectively. *Id.* Although 49.64 percent was the average contribution of property taxes relative to total municipal revenues, for some municipalities such as Hamilton, Medfield, and Concord, the percentage was as high as 75–80 percent. *See id.* at 4–5.

2. **Mass. Gen. Laws** ch. 59, § 21C. This initiative was originally passed in 1980. Mass. Acts 580.

3. The yearly levy limit is determined by applying (1) an automatic 2.5 percent increase over the prior fiscal year, (2) adding increases in total local property valuations resulting from growth, and (3) adding amounts authorized by limit override referendums. *See* **Massachusetts Department of Revenue, Division of Local Services, Levy Limits: A Primer on Proposition 2½** 5–6 (2001), available at http://www .dls.state.ma.us/PUBL/MISC/levylimits.pdf (last visited August 24, 2003) [hereinafter Levy Limits].

4. Certain limited capital projects costs can be added directly onto the levy limit by the local legislature without referendum approval. These include debts from water and sewer project and capital outlays for municipal loans to assist homeowners with the costs of repairs or replacements of faulty septic systems and the costs of removing underground fuel storage tanks and dangerous levels of lead paint in order to meet public health and safety code requirements. *See id.* at 12; **Mass. Gen. Laws** ch. 59, § 21C(n).

5. *See* Levy Limits, *supra* note 39, at 9–10; *see also* **Mass. Gen. Laws** ch. 59, § 21C(g) (overrides); **Mass. Gen. Laws** ch. 59, § 21C(i1/2) (capital exclusions); **Mass. Gen. Laws** ch. 59, § 21C(k) (debt exclusions).

6. *See* Jerome Saltzman & Brenda Buote, *Cities, Towns Keep Turning to Property Tax Overrides,* **Boston Globe,** July 2, 2003, at A1.

7. The success rate of Proposition 2½ referenda overrides vary from year to year, but averaged approximately 60 percent for the years 1993–2001. During that time, debt exclusions were the most successful category of overrides with a 73.7 percent success rate. General overrides, probably due to their compounding effects, were the least likely to be approved, with only 39.7 percent successful. *See* Department of Revenue, Division of Local Services, *Proposition 2 1/2 Referenda Trends,* **City and Town,** Nov./Dec. 2001, at 4–5.

8. *See* **Mass. Gen. Laws** ch. 40, § 56; *see also* **Charles K. Cobb, Tax Law in Massachusetts 1629–2000: A Primer for Taxpayers, Legislators and Lawyers** 81 (1999) ("Under present law cities and towns must revalue real and personal property every three years on a staggered schedule and have their revaluations approved

by the Commissioner of Revenue."); **Massachusetts Department of Revenue, Division of Local Services, A Guide to Financial Management for Town Officials** § 6.4, at 28 (2001) ("To ensure full and fair cash value assessments, the Department of Revenue certifies that a community's property valuations are at full value every three years through a certification process.").

9. *See* **Mass. Gen. Laws** ch. 59, § 23 ("No city, town or district tax rate for any fiscal year shall be fixed by the assessors until such rate has been approved by the commissioner.").

10. *See* **Massachusetts Department of Revenue**, *supra* note 44, § 6.1, at 27 ("The Department must approve the annual levy growth, Tax Recap Sheet, and set the tax rate before a community can issue its tax bills.").

11. There is a local option statute, made more generous in 2002, that authorizes municipalities to grant certain qualifying senior citizens an exemption from their property taxes. For a discussion of this provision and its parameters, see Kathleen Colleary, *Senior Property Tax Relief, City & Town*, **City and Town**, Nov./Dec. 2002, at 3, available at http://www.dls.state.ma.us/PUBL/CT/2002/nov_dec.pdf.

12. Rick Klein, *Fee Hikes Eyed to Aid Cities, Towns*, **Boston Globe**, July 8, 2003, page A-1.

13. *See Greater Franklin Developers v. Town of Franklin*, 49 Mass.App.Ct. 500, 505, 730 N.E.2d 900, 904 (2000).

14. *See FY01 Municipal Revenue Components*, *supra* note 37, at 3. These figures do not take into account state aid disbursements to regional school districts.

15. *See id.* at 4.

16. Massachusetts Department of Revenue, Division of Local Services, *Proposition 2 1/2—A Look Back*, **City and Town**, Nov./Dec. 2001, at 1, *available at* http://www.dls.state.ma.us/PUBL/CT/2001/Nov_Dec2.pdf.

17. The level of specificity and detail in chapter 40 extends to more than just regulating the type of funds that a municipality can create. For example, three provisions expressly permit localities to buy uniforms for local officials. Section 6B empowers municipalities to buy uniforms for the police and fire department and allows them to establish a clothing allowance fund for those departments. Section 6J extends uniform procurement authority by granting municipalities the power to purchase "stormy weather work clothes" for municipal employees. Section 6K covers uniforms for "public health nurses employed by its board of health." The state legislature thus empowered the municipalities to buy four different types of uniforms for their employees. Given the way that municipal home rule authority is interpreted, a court could find that these acts preempted an appropriation of funds for any other types of uniforms. *See* **Mass. Gen. Laws** ch. 40, §§ 6B, 6J, 6K.

18. **Mass. Gen. Laws** ch. 29, § 27C.

19. Town of Lexington v. Commissioner of Educ., 393 Mass. 693, 473 N.E.2d 673 (Mass. 1985) (Lexington I).

20. *School Comm. of Lexington v. Commissioner of Educ.*, 397 Mass. 593, 596, 492 N.E.2d 736, 737 (1986) (Lexington II).

21. *See* **Mass. Gen. Laws** ch. 70, §§ 2–3.

22. *See* Massachusetts Department of Revenue, Division of Local Services, *Fiscal Year 2002 General Fund Expenditures*, *at* http://www.dls.state.ma.us/MDMSTUF /MunicipalActualExpenditures/Expfn02.xls (last visited August 24, 2003).

Educational expenditures accounted for 48 percent of total municipal expenditures in Massachusetts. *See id.*

23. *See generally* **Mass. Gen. Laws** ch. 71B. Since the special education mandate was enacted prior to the "Local Mandate" provision passed in 1981, it was not subject to the restrictions set forth in **Mass. Gen. Laws** ch.29, § 27C. Nonetheless, Worcester challenged statutory and regulatory changes that were made to the special education mandate after 1981. The court, however, found that the amendment only clarified existing criteria of the mandate and did not impose new mandates. *City of Worcester v. The Governor*, 416 Mass. 751, 755–56, 625 N.E.2d 1337, 1340 (1994).

24. **Mass. Gen. Laws** ch. 71B, § 5A.

25. *See id.* at § 38Q.

26. *See id.* at ch. 15A, § 36.

27. *See* **Mass. Gen. Laws** ch. 149, § 34B (stating that all contracts related to public works and hiring reserve police officers will pay "the prevailing rate of wage paid to regular police officers in such city or town").

28. *id.* at §§ 26–27.

29. *See* **Cobb**, *supra* note 44, at 83.

CHAPTER 3

1. *Bd. of Appeals of Hanover v. Hous. Appeals Comm. in Dept. of Cmty. Affairs*, 363 Mass. 339, 359, 294 N.E.2d 393, 409 (1973).

2. *See id.*

3. Court interpretations seem to rely heavily on factual considerations in deciding whether a regulation is considered a "zoning" by-law or ordinance. These include an analysis of whether the municipality has passed similar regulations before as "zoning" regulations, how other municipalities have categorized similar regulations, and categorization of other, traditional types of regulations to which the present one can be analogized. *See, e.g., Rayco Inv. Corp. v. Bd. of Selectmen*, 368 Mass. 385, 393–94, 331 N.E.2d 910, 914 (1975) (holding a municipal by-law limiting the number of licenses that could be issued for trailer parks, and not pertaining to specific a parcel of land, to be a zoning by-law regulated by the Zoning Act); *Lovequist v. Conservation Comm. of Town of Dennis* 379 Mass. 7, 12, 393 N.E.2d 858, 862 (1979) (holding that a municipal wetland protection by-law requiring permission to alter or construct on specified protected wetlands is not a zoning bylaw, but a general bylaw enacted through the general police powers of the locality).

4. Codified in **Mass. Gen. Laws** ch. 41, §§ 81K–81GG.

5. Zoning Reform Working Group, *Some Facts About Land Use Law in Massachusetts*, (2002), at http://www.massapa.org/legislation.htm (last visited August 24, 2003).

6. **Mass. Gen. Laws** ch. 40A, § 3 ("No zoning ordinance or by-law shall regulate or restrict the interior area of a single family residential building . . . .").

7. *See* **Mass. Gen. Laws** ch. 41, § 81L (defining a "subdivision" to exclude those divisions whose lots retain frontage on, among other things, an existing public way); *id.* at § 81P (describing how a "subdivision" plan can acquire "approval not required" status if it can be demonstrated that the subdivision control law does not control).

8. *See* **Mass. Gen. Laws** ch. 40A, § 3.

9. *City of Medford v. Marinucci Bros. & Co.*, 344 Mass. 50, 54–55, 181 N.E.2d 584, 587 (1962).

10. *See id.* (finding a private party working for state exempt from zoning restriction even when the contract required compliance with all municipal regulations and ordinances).

11. *See New England Power Co. v. Board of Selectmen*, 389 Mass. 69, 77–78, 449 N.E.2d 648, 653 (1983).

12. *See Martorano v Department of Public Utilities*, 401 Mass. 257, 265, 516 N.E.2d 131, 136 (1987). Massachusetts regulations do require state agencies to report alternatives that take into account "applicable Federal, municipal, or regional plan" in their Environmental Impact Report. 301 CMR 11.07(6)(f)(3).

13. Executive Order 385 ("Planning for Growth).

14. Joel Russel, *Massachusetts Land-Use Law—Time for a Change*, **Land Use and Zoning Digest** Jan. 2002, at 3.

15. *See* **Mass. Gen. Laws** ch. 40A, § 5.

16. *See id.*

17. *See id.* at § 6.

18. *See* Russel, *supra* note 79, at 5 n.5.

19. The affordable housing requirements are contained in sections 19—23 of Chapter 40B.

20. Sharon Perlman Krefetz, *The Impact and Evolution of the Massachusetts Comprehensive Permit and Zoning Appeals Act: Thirty Years of Experience with a State Legislative Effort to Overcome Exclusionary Zoning*, 22 W. New Eng. L. Rev. 381, 392–94 (2001).

21. Sam Stonefield, *Affordable Housing in Suburbia: The Importance but Limited Power and Effectiveness of the State Override Tool*, 22 W. New Eng. L. Rev. 323, 327 (2001) ("Further, although the occupancy data is very incomplete, it seems the statutes have fostered little movement from city to suburb by lower-income families and less racial integration.").

22. *Bd. of Appeals of Hanover v. Hous. Appeals Comm. in the Dep't of Cmty. Affairs*, 363 Mass. 339, 359–60, 294 N.E.2d 393, 409 (1973).

23. *See* **Mass. Gen. Laws** ch, 40B, § 21.

24. *See id.* at §§ 22–23.

25. *Bd. of Appeals of Hanover*, 363 Mass. at 367, 294 N.E.2d at 413.

26. Krefetz, *supra* note 84, at 397–38. This includes petitions filed during 1970–1999. *See id.* at 398 n.82.

27. *See* **Mass. Gen. Laws** ch. 40B, § 20 (defining "Low or moderate income housing" as "any housing subsidized by the federal or state government under any program to assist the construction of low or moderate income housing as defined in the applicable federal or state statute").

28. *See id.*

29. A recent Supreme Judicial Court decision, *Zoning Board of Appeals of Wellesley v. Ardemore Apartments*, however, gives the locality a much stronger role in determining the length of time that the units must remain affordable. In *Ardemore*, the Zoning Board of Appeals in Wellesley granted a comprehensive permit for affordable housing construction to Ardemore, which had secured a loan from the state that

required the units to remain affordable for only fifteen years. 436 Mass. 811, 812–13, 767 N.E.2d 584, 586 (2002). Wellesley sued when Ardemore tried to covert these afforcable units to market price. The court found that "where a comprehensive permit itself does not specify for how long housing units must remain below market, the Act requires an owner to maintain the units as affordable for as long as the housing is not in compliance with local zoning requirements, regardless of the terms of any attendant construction subsidy agreements." *Id.* at 586, 813. The court also noted the importance of local autonomy when balanced with the interests of the state for affordable units: "We see nothing in the Act to suggest that the Legislature intended to override local zoning autonomy only to create a fleeting increase in affordable housing stock, leaving cities and towns vulnerable to successive zoning overrides, and the issuance of a never-ending series of comprehensive permits." *Id.*

30. *See* Krefetz, *supra* note 84, at 409.

31. *Marshal House v. Rent Review and Grievance Board of Brookline*, 357 Mass. 709, 718, 260 N.E.2d 200, 207 (1976).

32. C842

33. *Flynn v. City of Cambridge*, 383 Mass. 152, 159, 418 N.E.2d 335, 339 (1981).

34. *Steinbergh v. Rent Control Bd. of Cambridge*, 406 Mass. 147, 151–52, 546 N.E.2d 169, 172 (1989).

35. *See* 1994 Mass. Acts 282 (codified in **Mass. Gen. Laws** ch. 40P).

36. *Greater Boston Real Estate Board v. City of Boston*, 428 Mass. 797, 800–01, 705 N.E.2d 256, 258 (1999).

37. See *Bannerman v. City of Fall River*, 391 Mass. 328, 330–31, 461 N.E.2d 793, 795 (1984); *CHR General, Inc. v. City of Newton*, 387 Mass. 351, 354, 439 N.E.2d 788, 790 (1982).

38. *Middlesex & Boston Street Ry. Co. v. Bd. of Aldermen of Newton*, 371 Mass. 849, 856–57, 359 N.E.2d 1279, 1283 (1977).

39. *See Id.* at 858, 1284.

40. **Mass. Gen. Laws** ch. 40A, § 9.

41. *See* **Mass. Gen. Laws** ch. 44B.

42. *See id.* at § 10.

43. State-wide spending under the Community Preservation Act from 2002 to 2003 saw a significant increase in the funds directed towards affordable housing. Much of this increase, however, is due to housing projects in the City of Cambridge. Spending on affordable housing was 28 percent, and open space was 54 percent, of total state-wide spending in 2002. In 2003, the tables were essentially turned, with affordable housing accounting for 50 percent of total spending and open space accounting for 25 percent. If the City of Cambridge, which had just adopted the Act, is excluded from the equation, only 36 percent of total expenditures in 2003 went to affordable housing, while the open space percentage jumps to 34 percent. *See* Community Preservation Act Coalition, *CPA Projects in 2002 and 2003*, at http://www.communitypreservation.org/CPAProjectlist.htm (last checked September 25, 2003). Furthermore, out of the current Community Preservation projects underway, 286 units of affordable housing are being developed compared to 1,616 acres of open space acquisitions. *See id.*

44. The Community Preservation Act is only available to municipalities that accept it through a ballot question. *See* **Mass. Gen. Laws** ch. 44B, § 3.

45. *See* Trust for Public Land, *Status of Community Preservation Act Implementation*, at http://www.tpl.org/content_documents/CPA_votes_as_of_5-20-03.xls (last modified May 20, 2003). In several communities, the final action is still pending. *See id.*

CHAPTER 4

1. The Massachusetts Comprehensive Assessment System is a state-wide testing requirement administered to students which determines grade advancement and ultimately whether a student can graduate with a high school diploma. It was instituted along with the Massachusetts Education Reform Act. *See* **Mass. Gen. Laws** ch. 69, § 1I; Mass. Regs. Code tit. 603, § 30.00 (2002).

2. Michele Kurtz, *MCAS Part of Deciding on a Town*, **Boston Globe**, September, 24, 2002, at B.1.

3. **Massachusetts Education Reform Review Commission, 2002 Annual Report on the Progress of Education Reform in Massachusetts, Executive Summary**, at v [Hereafter 2002 Annual Report].

4. **Myron Orfield et al., Boston Metropatterns: A Regional Agenda for Community and Stability in Greater Boston 16 (2001).**

5. *Id.*

6. The powers, duties, and responsibilities of school committees are outlined in **Mass. Gen. Laws** ch. 71, §§ 35–67. Special concerns relating to regional school committees are addressed by *id.* at § 16A.

7. *Leonard v. School Comm. of the City of Springfield*, 241 Mass. 325, 329, 135 N.E. 459, 461 (1922). School committees are generally "not subject to the review by any other board of tribunal," but they are not exempt from challenges from their constituents. A school committee decision may be rescinded by referendum. *See Moore v. School Comm. of Newton*, 375 Mass. 443, 447, 378 N.E.2d 47, 50 (1978).

8. This circumstance does not necessarily have to be the case, though state law helps to assure that it is the norm. **Mass. Gen. Laws.** ch. 71, § 37M allows municipalities, upon the consent of the majority vote of both the school committee and the municipal legislature, to consolidate the "administrative functions . . . of the school committee with the city or town." None of the municipalities interviewed reported having done so in their community, perhaps in part because the state statutes gives the school committee power to veto a municipal government's attempt to diminish its independence.

9. **Mass. Gen. Laws** ch. 71, § 34. In regional school districts, the regional school committee proposes the general operating budget, which is then apportioned to the individual localities in a manner determined by their initial agreement. All participating municipalities must approve that apportionment. If they do not, the regional school district has to submit another proposal that reapportions the budget to all the municipalities involved. Options are also provided for situations where a participating municipality continues to reject a proposal. If there are only two participating municipality, the school committee can call a district wide meeting and attempt to get a majority vote of all participating registered voters. Impasses involving school districts with more than two municipalities allow the Department of Education to set its own budget determination and assume the operation of the schools, deducting the appropriate amount from all the municipality's local aid distribution. *See id.* at §16B.

10. The statute that created the new Boston School Committee is 1991 Mass. Acts 108.

11. *See McDuffy v. Sec'y of the Executive Office of Ed.*, 415 Mass. 545, 606, 615 N.E.2d 516, 548 (1993).

12. This foundation level is only a minimum. Local districts are entitled to add to this amount, with their ability to do so very much influenced by their property tax rate. As the 2002 Report puts it, "the level of effort is lowest for the highest-income category and highest for the second-lowest income category." 2002 Annual Report, *supra* note 113, at vi.

13. *See* **Mass. Gen. Laws** ch. 69, §§ 1D, 1E. The Current frameworks can be found at http://www.coe.mass.edu/frameworks/current.html.

14. **Mass. Gen. Laws** ch. 71, §§ 2, 3.

15. **Mass. Gen. Laws** ch. 69, §§ 1G, 1J.

16. 20 U.S.C. § 6301 (2002).

17. **Mass. Gen. Laws** ch.69, § 1I.

18. Brenda J. Buote, *MCAS at Critical Juncture: Local Schools Face Graduation Decision*, Boston Globe (**Globe North**), Sept. 12, 2002, at 1.

19. *Id.* (internal quotation marks omitted).

20. Criticisms of the MCAS range from its failure to address inadequate school preparation, its disparate impact on students from families of limited means and on racial minorities, and the structure and subject matters of the test itself. *See, e g.,* Anand Vaishnav, *Lawsuit to allege MCAS is Widely Discriminatory*, **Boston Globe**, Sept. 19, 2002, at A1. Commentators have also criticized the test for discouraging students and increasing school drop-outs at earlier grades. *See, e.g.,* Clive McFarlane, *Rising dropout rate blurs MCAS figures; Failing students may have given up*, **Telegram & Gazette (Worcester, MA)**, Sept. 16, 2002, at A1. *But see* Michele Kurtz, *State Says MCAS Produced no Jump in Dropout Rates*, **Boston Globe**, Aug. 27, 2002, at A1.

21. The funds are conditioned upon approval by the State Board of Education pursuant to certain established criteria. *See generally* **Mass. Gen. Laws** ch. 703. Nevertheless, there has been criticism that Massachusetts' complex bidding statute dealing with public construction projects adds costs to school construction projects without producing significant gains in construction quality. *See* **Mass. Gen. Laws** ch. 149, §§ 44A–44H.

22. *See* Cambridge Public School District, Controlled Choice Plan (Superintendent Recommendation #01–168), December 18, 2001, available at http://204.167.95.13/NewFiles/final.pdf; Steve LeBlanc, *Cambridge, Massachusetts, to desegregate schools based on economics instead of race*, Associated Press, Jan. 11, 2002. The desegregation plan applies only to Cambridge's elementary school students. *See id.*

23. *See* **Mass. Gen. Laws** ch. 76, § 12B. School committees are allowed, after a public hearing, to decide not to accept out-of-district students. *See id.*

24. *See* 2002 Annual Report, *supra* note 113, at ii.

25. Charter schools are governed by **Mass. Gen. Laws** ch. 71, § 89.

26. *See id.* at § 89(a)

27. *See id.* at § 89(b). A recent statutory amendment now permits one school committee member to sit on the board of trustees for a Horace Mann charter school. *See id.*

28. At the same time, charter school advocates have complained that the current funding formula does little to assist them in raising the start-up capital needed to create the infrastructure for a new school.
29. *See id.* at § 89(ff).
30. *Id.* at § 89(kk).

CHAPTER 5

1. Metropolitan Area Planning Council, *Metro Area*, at http://www.mapc.org/metro_area.html (last visited August 25, 2003).
2. *See* **Mass. Gen. Laws** ch. 71, § 15.
3. *See, e.g.,* **Mass. Gen. Laws** ch. 40N, § 25 (regional water and sewer district commission); *id.* at ch. 71, § 15 (regional school districts); *id.* at ch. 41, § 99C (regional police district); *id* at ch. 161B, § 3 (regional transit authority); *id,* at ch. 34B, § 20 (regional charter commission).
4. Telecom City was not the first project to receive special state legislation empowering multiple municipalities to form a commission and collectively decide how to develop a specific parcel of land. Prior to Telecom City, two such commissions were formed to handle the redevelopment of decommissioned military installations in Massachusetts. *See* 1993 Mass. Acts 498 (redevelopment of Fort Devens); 1998 Mass. Acts 301 (redevelopment of South Weymouth Naval Air Station).
5. Home Rule Amendment, Mass. Const. art. LXXXIX, § 8.